MEECH LAKE CONSTITUTIONAL ACCORD ANNOTATED

◆

Peter W. Hogg
Q.C.,LL.B.,LL.M.,Ph.D.
PROFESSOR OF LAW, OSGOODE HALL LAW SCHOOL
YORK UNIVERSITY, TORONTO

CARSWELL
Toronto ▪ Calgary ▪ Vancouver
1988

Canadian Cataloguing in Publication Data

Hogg, Peter W.
   Meech Lake Constitutional Accord annotated

Supplement to: Hogg, Peter W. Constitutional law
of Canada.   2nd ed.
Includes appendices in French and English.
ISBN 0-459-31471-8 (bound)   ISBN 0-459-31481-5 (pbk.)

1. Canada. Constitution Act, 1982.   2. Canada -
Constitutional law - Amendments. . . . Federal-
provincial relations - Canada.*   4. Federal
government - Canada.   I. Hogg, Peter W.
Constitutional law of Canada. 2nd ed.   II. Title.

KE4219.H632   1988   342.71'03   C88-093282-1
KF4482.H642   1988

PREFACE

This little book is an annotation of the Meech Lake Constitutional Accord, which is the set of amendments to the Constitution of Canada that were agreed to in principle by the Prime Minister and the ten provincial Premiers meeting at Meech Lake, Quebec, on April 30, 1987. The detailed text of the Accord was settled at a second meeting of the first ministers at the Langevin Block, Ottawa, on June 3, 1987. The Accord as settled at the latter meeting, consists of three documents: (1) the political accord, (2) the motion for a resolution, and (3) the schedule to the resolution. All three documents are reproduced and analyzed, but it is the last document that contains the text of the proposed amendments and to which most of the book is devoted. The Meech Lake communiqué of April 30, 1987 and the three documents agreed to on June 3, 1987 are set out, in both English and French, in four appendices.

The purpose of the book is to provide students of law with an explanation of the constitutional changes proposed by the Accord. At the time of writing it appears very likely indeed that the Accord will be ratified by the eleven legislative bodies required by the applicable amending formula. The Accord has reconciled the government of Quebec to the Constitution Act, 1982. Nevertheless, in some quarters the Accord is controversial. It is criticized (mainly in Ontario) for ceding too many powers to the provinces. It is criticized (mainly in Quebec) for ceding insufficient powers to the province of Quebec. It is criticized (mainly by women's groups) for not reaffirming the principle of sexual equality. It is criticized (mainly in the territories) for making it more difficult for a territory to achieve provincial status. Other criticisms have been made. It will inevitably emerge from my commentary that I do not believe that the Accord effects major changes in our constitutional law or practice, so that I cannot accept the predictions of doom that are made by some critics. However, it is not my intention to add to the political controversy. I have confined myself to providing a legal exegesis of the text of the proposed amendments. Obviously, there is room for argument as to whether I am correct in my interpretations, but I do not enter upon any criticism or suggest any changes to the Accord. I take it as it emerged from the first ministers' meeting on June 3, 1987.

My motive in publishing this annotation is to supplement the second edition of my book, *Constitutional Law of Canada* (Carswell, 2nd ed., 1985). While the annotation is not written in the form of a supplement, it is designed to postpone the distressingly rapid obsolescence of the second edition, and provide an excuse for further delay in preparing a third edition. This book thus serves a similar function to my *Canada Act 1982 Annotated* (Carswell, 1982), which I published as quickly as I could after the constitutional settlement of 1982. The latter book was eventually superseded by a new edition of *Constitutional Law of Canada*. The same fate awaits this work as well.

An earlier version of part of chapter 8, Spending Provision, was delivered as a paper at the Symposium on the Meech Lake Accord held at the University of Toronto on October 30, 1987. Those papers are to be published in a volume edited by Professors Katherine Swinton and Carol Rogerson.

I served as a member of the Constitutional Advisory Committee of the Government of Ontario, which provided advice to the Deputy Minister of Intergovernmental Affairs and to the Premier (who was also the Minister of Intergovernmental Affairs) during the one-year period of the Quebec round of constitutional discussions that culminated in the Meech Lake Constitutional Accord. This book is not concerned with the political events of the period. Nor does the book have any official status. The legal opinions expressed are entirely my own, and are not necessarily shared by the law officers and other officials of the government of Ontario.

Toronto
December 3, 1987   Peter W. Hogg

CONTENTS

TABLE OF CASES

1

HISTORY

Meech Lake Accord

The Meech Lake Constitutional Accord was reached by the Prime Minister and the ten Premiers on April 30, 1987 at Meech Lake, Quebec. The Accord consisted of an agreement on a group of constitutional amendments. The purpose of the Accord was to better accommodate Quebec within the Canadian federation. The actual text of the constitutional amendments agreed to at Meech Lake was settled at a second meeting of the eleven first ministers on June 3, 1987 in the Langevin Block, a federal building in Ottawa. It is this text that is set out and analyzed in this volume. This text will hereafter be described as the Meech Lake Constitutional Accord.

In order to become law, the Meech Lake Constitutional Accord has to be ratified by resolutions of the Senate and House of Commons and of the legislative assembly of each province. This "unanimity" procedure is required by s. 41 of the Constitution Act, 1982, because the amendments include provisions relating to the composition of the Supreme Court of Canada (s. 41(d)) and a change in the amending procedures (s. 41(e)). At the time of writing (1987), this process is not far advanced. On June 23, 1987, Quebec's legislative assembly passed the required resolution of approval. On June 16 and 17, 1987, the Senate and House of Commons established a Special Joint Committee on the 1987 Constitutional Accord, which held hearings and produced a report in September 1987. The report recommended that the Senate and House of Commons pass the required resolution of approval: Special Joint Committee of the Senate and of the House of Commons on the 1987 Constitutional Accord, *Report*, (1987). At the time of writing that resolution has been passed by the House of Commons (October 26, 1987), but not by the Senate. On September 24, 1987, Saskatchewan's legislative assembly passed a resolution of approval. Quebec and Saskatchewan are the only provinces that have yet passed the required resolution of approval.

The Report of the Special Joint Committee referred to above is a very useful analysis of the Accord. It will be referred to in the commentary on the Accord that follows.

Quebec referendum

The roots of the Meech Lake Constitutional Accord may be found in the Quebec referendum on sovereignty-association which was held by Quebec's Parti Québécois government on May 20, 1980. The referendum was defeated by a popular vote of 60 per cent to 40 per cent. In the referendum campaign the federalist forces promised that a "no" to sovereignty-association was not a vote for the status quo, and the defeat of the referendum would be followed by constitutional change to better accommodate Quebec's aspirations.

Constitution Act, 1982

The defeat of the Quebec referendum was immediately followed by a series of constitutional conferences in the summer and early fall of 1980, but these conferences failed to yield agreement on the specifics of constitutional change. On October 6, 1980, despite the absence of a federal-provincial agreement, Prime Minister Trudeau introduced in the federal House of Commons a resolution calling for a set of constitutional amendments to accomplish at least the patriation of the Constitution, the adoption of an amending procedure, and the adoption of a charter of rights. This resolution was debated and amended and eventually passed by the House of Commons and the Senate in April 1981.

Only two provinces — Ontario and New Brunswick — agreed with the federal resolution. The other eight provinces were opposed, and they obtained a ruling from the Supreme Court of Canada to the effect that the federal government would be in breach of a constitutional convention if it proceeded with the amendments without having first secured a "substantial degree" of provincial consent: *Re Resolution to Amend the Constitution* [1981] 1 S.C.R. 753. After this ruling, a new round of discussions at last yielded an agreement on an altered package of amendments. The agreement was reached between the Prime Minister and the Premiers of all provinces except Quebec on November 5, 1981. This agreement, supplemented by several changes agreed to shortly thereafter, was embodied in a resolution that passed the federal Parliament in December 1981, and was enacted by the Parliament of the United Kingdom in March 1982. The outcome of this process was the Canada Act 1982 (which terminated the United Kingdom Parliament's authority over Canada) and the Constitution Act, 1982 (which contained the substantive amendments to the Constitution of Canada). The Constitution Act, 1982 was proclaimed in force in Canada on April 17, 1982.

The Constitution Act, 1982 was a major achievement, curing several long-standing defects in the Constitution of Canada. The Constitution could now be amended within Canada without recourse to the United Kingdom (ss. 38-49). The Constitution now included a Charter of Rights, which included language rights for the French-speaking minority (and the English-speaking minority in Quebec) (ss. 1-34). Aboriginal rights were recognized (s. 35). Equalization was guaranteed (s. 36). Provincial powers over natural resources were extended (ss. 50, 51). A supremacy clause was adopted (s. 52). Provision was made for the translation of the English-only parts of the Constitution into French (ss. 55-57).

The Constitution Act, 1982 failed to accomplish one of the goals of the constitutional discussions that had followed the Quebec referendum, and that was the better accommodation of Quebec within the Canadian federation. The Premier of Quebec had been the sole dissenter at the federal-provincial meeting of November 5, 1981. In fact, the government of Quebec directed a reference to the courts for a ruling that it would be a breach of a constitutional convention to proceed with the amendments without the consent of the province of Quebec. The Supreme Court of Canada eventually ruled that Quebec had no such conventional veto: *Re Objection by Quebec to Resolution to Amend the Constitution* [1982] 2 S.C.R. 793. But the fact remained that Quebec had not agreed to a set of constitutional changes that had the effect of diminishing the powers of the Legislature and government of Quebec. The new amending procedures did not give a veto to Quebec, something which had in the past always been recognized in practice. And the new Charter of Rights restricted the powers of the provincial Legislatures, and, in particular, as the Supreme Court of Canada later held, the Charter rendered unconstitutional the "Quebec clause" of Quebec's law restricting admission to English-language schools: *A.-G. Que. v. Quebec Protestant School Boards* [1984] 2 S.C.R. 66. Thus, the outcome of the constitutional changes of 1982 was a diminution of Quebec's powers and a profound sense of grievance in the province.

Aftermath of Constitution Act, 1982

Quebec was, of course, legally bound by the Constitution Act, 1982, because the Act had been adopted into law by the correct constitutional procedures. However, the government of Quebec thereafter refused to participate in constitutional changes that involved the new amending procedures. And the government "opted out" of the new Charter of Rights to the maximum extent possible under s. 33 by introducing a "notwithstanding clause" into each of its existing statutes, and into every newly-enacted statute. As well as these practical measures, politicians, journalists and intellectuals of all political persuasions kept alive the notion that the Constitution Act, 1982 lacked political legitimacy in the province of Quebec.

In 1984 changes occurred in the federal government. Prime Minister Trudeau resigned on June 30, 1984, and was replaced by a new Liberal leader, Mr. Turner, who became Prime Minister until the federal election on September 4, 1984. In that election, the Liberals were defeated, and the Progressive Conservative government of Prime Minister Mulroney took office. One of the new government's policies was to achieve a reconciliation with Quebec.

In 1985 changes occurred in the Quebec government. On December 2, 1985 a provincial election was held, and the Parti Québécois government was defeated. The new Liberal government of Premier Bourassa continued the non-participation policy of the previous government, but it also moved to seek a reconciliation with the rest of Canada. The government announced five conditions that were required for Quebec's acceptance of the Constitution Act, 1982. These were: (1) recognition of Quebec as a distinct society; (2) a greater provincial role in immigration; (3) a provincial role in appointments to the Supreme Court of Canada; (4) limitations on the federal spending power; and (5) a veto for Quebec on constitutional amendments.

The Prime Minister and the other provincial Premiers agreed to negotiate on Quebec's five conditions. The outcome of those negotiations was the Meech Lake Constitutional Accord. For the first time in Canadian history an answer had been provided to the question: what does Quebec want? The Accord reconciles the government of Quebec to the Constitution Act, 1982, so that it will henceforth participate in future constitutional change, and will no longer attempt routinely to override the Charter of Rights. Perhaps even more importantly, a sense of grievance flowing from Quebec's exclusion from the agreement of November 5, 1981 has been erased or at least mitigated.

What follows in this volume is the text of the Accord with explanatory notes after each of the provisions. Technically, the Accord consists of three documents: (1) the political accord, (2) the motion for a resolution, and (3) the schedule to the resolution, which contains the text of the proposed amendments.

2

POLITICAL ACCORD

Text of accord

The first of the three documents comprising the Meech Lake Constitutional Accord is the "political accord", which provides as follows:

1987 CONSTITUTIONAL ACCORD

WHEREAS first ministers, assembled in Ottawa, have arrived at a unanimous accord on constitutional amendments that would bring about the full and active participation of Quebec in Canada's constitutional evolution, would recognize the principle of equality of all the provinces, would provide new arrangements to foster greater harmony and cooperation between the Government of Canada and the governments of the provinces and would require that annual first ministers' conferences on the state of the Canadian economy and such other matters as may be appropriate be convened and that annual constitutional conferences composed of first ministers be convened commencing not later than December 31, 1988;

AND WHEREAS first ministers have also reached unanimous agreement on certain additional commitments in relation to some of those amendments;

NOW THEREFORE the Prime Minister of Canada and the first ministers of the provinces commit themselves and the governments they represent to the following:

1. The Prime Minister of Canada will lay or cause to be laid before the Senate and House of Commons, and the first ministers of the provinces will lay or cause to be laid before their legislative assemblies, as soon as possible, a resolution, in the form appended hereto, to authorize a proclamation to be issued by the Governor General under the Great Seal of Canada to amend the Constitution of Canada.

2. The Government of Canada will, as soon as possible, conclude an agreement with the Government of Quebec that would

(*a*) incorporate the principles of the Cullen-Couture agreement on the selection abroad and in Canada of independent immigrants, visitors for medical treatment, students and temporary workers, and on the selection of refugees abroad and economic criteria for family reunification and assisted relatives,

(*b*) guarantee that Quebec will receive a number of immigrants, including refugees, within the annual total established by the federal government for all of Canada proportionate to its share of the population of Canada, with the right to exceed that figure by five per cent for demographic reasons, and

(*c*) provide an undertaking by Canada to withdraw services (except citizenship services) for the reception and integration (including linguistic and cultural) of all foreign nationals wishing to settle in Quebec where services are to be provided by Quebec, with such withdrawal to be accompanied by reasonable compensation,

and the Government of Canada and the Government of Quebec will take the necessary steps to give the agreement the force of law under the proposed amendment relating to such agreements.

3. Nothing in this Accord should be construed as preventing the negotiation of similar agreements with other provinces relating to immigration and the temporary admission of aliens.

4. Until the proposed amendment relating to appointments to the Senate comes into force, any person summoned to fill a vacancy in the Senate shall be chosen from among persons whose names have been submitted by the government of the province to which the vacancy relates and must be acceptable to the Queen's Privy Council for Canada.

Ratification process

The political accord recites the fact that the first ministers have reached agreement on the Meech Lake Constitutional Accord. It contains an undertaking that the Prime Minister and each of the Premiers will proceed with the process of ratification by the Parliament and Legislatures that is required by s. 41 of the Constitution Act, 1982.

Interim measures

The political accord contains two undertakings that may be carried out before the ratification process is complete. One is an undertaking by the government of Canada to enter into an agreement with the government of Quebec regarding immigration into Quebec. This agreement would be one of a kind contemplated by clause 3 of the Accord, which is discussed in chapter 6, Immigration, below.

The other undertaking, also by the government of Canada, is to make appointments to the Senate from names submitted by the provinces. This mode of appointment is stipulated by clause 2 of the Accord, which is discussed in chapter 5, Senate, below. The purpose of this undertaking is to put the new procedure in place immediately without waiting for ratification by the eleven legislative bodies.

3

MOTION FOR A RESOLUTION

Text of motion

The second of the three documents comprising the Meech Lake Constitutional Accord is the "motion for a resolution", which provides as follows:

MOTION FOR A RESOLUTION TO AUTHORIZE AN AMENDMENT TO THE CONSTITUTION OF CANADA

WHEREAS the *Constitution Act, 1982* came into force on April 17, 1982, following an agreement between Canada and all the provinces except Quebec;

AND WHEREAS the Government of Quebec has established a set of five proposals for constitutional change and has stated that amendments to give effect to those proposals would enable Quebec to resume a full role in the constitutional councils of Canada;

AND WHEREAS the amendment proposed in the schedule hereto sets out the basis on which Quebec's five constitutional proposals may be met;

AND WHEREAS the amendment proposed in the schedule hereto also recognizes the principle of the equality of all the provinces, provides new arrangements to foster greater harmony and cooperation between the Government of Canada and the governments of the provinces and requires that conferences be convened to consider important constitutional, economic and other issues;

AND WHEREAS certain portions of the amendment proposed in the schedule hereto relate to matters referred to in section 41 of the *Constitution Act, 1982*;

AND WHEREAS section 41 of the *Constitution Act, 1982* provides that an amendment to the Constitution of Canada may be made by proclamation issued by the Governor General under the Great Seal of Canada where so authorized by resolutions of the Senate and the House of Commons and of the legislative assembly of each province;

NOW THEREFORE the (Senate) (House of Commons) (legislative assembly) resolves that an amendment to the Constitution of Canada be authorized to be made by proclamation issued by Her Excellency the Governor General under the Great Seal of Canada in accordance with the schedule hereto.

Purpose of motion

The motion for a resolution is the formal instrument that is to be approved by the Senate, the House of Commons and the provincial legislative assemblies. Once approval of all these bodies has been obtained, the amendment is proclaimed into force by the Governor General. That is the procedure contemplated by s. 41 of the Constitution Act, 1982.

The actual text of the proposed constitutional amendments is contained in the "schedule" that is referred to in the last line of the motion. That schedule is the third of the three documents comprising the Meech Lake Constitutional Accord. There are seventeen clauses to the schedule. Each is set out below, under an appropriate heading, and followed by some explanatory commentary.

4

DUALISM AND DISTINCT SOCIETY

Text of s. 2

Clause 1 of the schedule to the Meech Lake Constitutional Accord will add a new s. 2 to the Constitution Act, 1867. (The original s. 2 was repealed in 1893.) The new s. 2 provides as follows:

Interpretation

2. (1) The Constitution of Canada shall be interpreted in a manner consistent with

(a) the recognition that the existence of French-speaking Canadians, centred in Quebec but also present elsewhere in Canada, and English-speaking Canadians, concentrated outside Quebec but also present in Quebec, constitutes a fundamental characteristic of Canada; and

(b) The recognition that Quebec constitutes within Canada a distinct society.

Role of Parliament and legislatures

(2) The role of the Parliament of Canada and the provincial legislatures to preserve the fundamental characteristic of Canada referred to in paragraph (1)(a) is affirmed.

Role of legislature and Government of Quebec

(3) The role of the legislature and Government of Quebec to preserve and promote the distinct identity of Quebec referred to in paragraph (1)(b) is affirmed.

Rights of legislatures and governments preserved

(4) Nothing in this section derogates from the powers, rights or privileges of Parliament or the Government of Canada, or of the legislatures or

governments of the provinces, including any powers, rights or privileges relating to language.

This text must be read with clause 16 of the schedule to the Accord, which provides as follows:

Multicultural heritage and aboriginal peoples

16. Nothing in section 2 of the *Constitution Act, 1867* affects section 25 or 27 of the *Canadian Charter of Rights and Freedoms*, section 35 of the *Constitution Act, 1982* or class 24 of section 91 of the *Constitution Act, 1867*.

Clauses 1 and 16 of the schedule to the Accord are discussed in the *Report* of the Special Joint Committee on the 1987 Constitutional Accord (1987), chs. V, VI.

Rule of interpretation

Subsection (1) of s. 2 provides that the Constitution is to be interpreted in a manner consistent with the recognition of (a) the existence of linguistic duality in Canada and (b) the fact that Quebec constitutes a "distinct society". Subsection (1) is expressly an interpretation provision. It neither confers power nor denies power. It will be relevant only where other constitutional provisions are unclear or ambiguous, and where reference to the ideas of linguistic duality or distinct society would help to clarify the meaning. It is difficult to identify constitutional provisions that are unclear or ambiguous in that way. Subsection (1) should probably be seen as an affirmation of sociological facts with little legal significance.

Subsection (2) of s. 2 provides that the "role" of the Parliament of Canada and the provincial legislatures to "preserve" the fundamental characteristic of Canada referred to in paragraph (1)(a) (that is, linguistic duality) is "affirmed". And subsection (3) provides that the "role" of the Legislature and government of Quebec to "preserve and promote" the "distinct identity of Quebec" is "affirmed". A faint argument could perhaps be made that these provisions are new grants of power. But the words "role" and "affirmed" are not words that are used elsewhere in the Constitution to confer power. The better view is that subsections (2) and (3) simply recognize each jurisdiction's existing powers. Both levels of government possess considerable powers over language, and are in a position to preserve linguistic duality. Quebec, in common with the other provinces, possesses considerable powers over language, education, property and civil rights and other cultural matters, and is in a position "to preserve and promote the distinct identity of Quebec". (As to the source and extent of these powers, see Hogg, *Constitutional Law of Canada* (2nd ed., 1985), especially chapters 20 (property and civil rights), 36 (language) and 37 (education).) It is within the framework of these existing powers that subsections (2) and (3) affirm the roles of the Parliament, the provincial Legislatures, and the Legislature and government of Quebec. Like subsection (1), subsections (2) and (3) are affirmations of the facts of Canada's linguistic duality and Quebec's distinctness, which in unusual cases could serve as interpretative aids, but which have little direct legal significance.

Subsection (4) of s. 2 is a cautionary provision designed to make clear that in no event should subsections (1) to (3) be given the effect of reducing the powers, rights or privileges of the Parliament or government of Canada or the Legislatures or governments of the provinces. Subsection (4) says nothing about increasing the powers of the two levels of government. That omission is discussed later in this chapter, under the heading "Distribution of powers".

Distinct society

There would be general agreement that, as a matter of fact, Quebec constitutes within Canada a "distinct society". It is not, however, easy to define the characteristics that make Quebec distinct, and the Accord makes no attempt to do so. The most obvious one is the existence of a French-speaking majority: Quebec is unique among the provinces in that respect. However, Quebec is not an exclusively French-speaking society: there is a substantial English-speaking minority. The presence in Quebec of the English-speaking minority is expressly recognized by s. 2(1)(a), and the role of the Quebec Legislature in preserving that minority is affirmed by s. 2(2). It is plain, therefore, from the text of s. 2 that Quebec's distinct society is one in which French and English coexist.

Language is only part of a distinct culture in Quebec which has its roots in French colonial history. This is why Quebec is the only province with a system of civil law instead of common law. Its civil procedure is quite different from that of the other provinces. Beyond language and law, Quebec's distinctness finds expression in a host of public and private institutions that are unlike their equivalents in the other provinces.

While the "distinct society" clause by itself is mainly hortatory or symbolic, the Meech Lake Accord does go on to give concrete expression to the idea. The new immigration provisions (ss. 95A to 95E) give constitutional status to immigration agreements with individual provinces, which will enable Quebec to participate in the selection of its own immigrants, giving appropriate weight to their capacity to settle in a predominantly French-speaking community. The new Supreme Court of Canada provisions (ss. 101A to 101E) guarantee that at least three of the judges must come from Quebec (s. 101B(2)), thereby ensuring that a core of judges is familiar with Quebec's unique system of civil law. And, of course, the provisions for a provincial role in the selection of Supreme Court judges (s. 101C), the limitation of the federal spending power (s. 106A) and the changes to the amending procedures (ss. 40-41), although applicable to all provinces, were driven by Quebec's concern to protect its society from national interference.

Distinct society elsewhere

The recognition of Quebec as a distinct society is not unique to the Meech Lake Constitutional Accord. The Constitution Act, 1867 created a federal state rather than a unitary state primarily because of the concern of French-Canadians to protect a distinct society in the territory of Quebec. That is an historical fact, never explicitly acknowledged in the language of the Constitution Act, 1867. But the Act does contain several provisions that in effect give recognition to the distinctness of Quebec.

With respect to language, s. 133 of the Constitution Act, 1867 provides a guarantee of the use of both the English and French languages in the federal courts, and in the Quebec Legislature and Quebec courts. The guarantee does not apply in the other founding provinces. A similar guarantee was extended to Manitoba when it was created in 1870: at that time, Manitoba had a French majority which feared that it would be swamped by English-speaking immigration; the guarantee is in s. 23 of the Manitoba Act, 1870. In 1982, ss. 16 to 20 of the Charter of Rights extended a similar guarantee to New Brunswick. But no similar guarantee applies in the other seven provinces.

With respect to law, s. 94 of the Constitution Act, 1867 authorizes the federal Parliament to make provision for the uniformity of laws relative to property and civil rights and civil procedure in Ontario, Nova Scotia and New Brunswick. This provision has never been used. What is interesting about s. 94, however, is that it contemplates uniform laws in only three of the four founding provinces. (Its scope now extends to the nine common law provinces.) Plainly, the assumption was that Quebec's Civil Code and Code of Civil Procedure would remain distinct from the comparable laws in the common law provinces. That is, of course, exactly what has happened.

Another example — less clear than the others — is religion. Section 93 of the Constitution Act, 1867 confers upon the provincial Legislatures the power to make laws in relation to education. Section 93(1) limits that power by guaranteeing denominational school rights in existence at the union. Section 93(2) applies only to Quebec, extending the denominational school rights in existence in Upper Canada at the union to "the dissentient schools of the Queen's Protestant and Roman Catholic subjects in Quebec". Once again, special provision is made to meet the special situation of Quebec.

Thus, while the Constitution of Canada recognizes in a general way the equality of the provinces, equality has never been a hard-and-fast rule, and the Constitution often recognizes that differences of history and geography call for different treatment of provinces. This applies not only to Quebec. Language and denominational school rights differ in other provinces as well. Indeed, the terms upon which each new province was admitted have usually included terms unique to that province; those terms have constitutional status: *The Queen Can. v. The Queen P.E.I.* (1977) 83 D.L.R. (3d) 492 (Fed. C.A.) (enforcing term of union promising ferry service); *Jack v. The Queen* [1980] 1 S.C.R. 294 (interpreting term of union regarding policy towards Indians); *Moosehunter v. The Queen* [1981] 1 S.C.R. 282 (enforcing term of natural resources agreement guaranteeing Indian hunting rights).

Distribution of powers

The new s. 2 will have no significant impact on the distribution of powers between the federal Parliament and the provincial Legislatures. A long chain of jurisprudence has settled the main lines of demarcation between the federal and the provincial spheres. There remain "grey areas" where the demarcation is uncertain, and it is conceivable that recourse to the interpretative ideas of linguistic duality and distinct society may help to clarify some points. But the room for s. 2 to contribute to the process of interpretation seems small.

Subsection (4) of the new s. 2 has a bearing on this issue as well. Subsection (4) provides that nothing in s. 2 derogates from the powers of the federal Parliament or the provincial Legislatures. Since most of the legislative powers conferred on the federal Parliament or the provincial Legislatures are exclusive, it is usually the case that an increase in the powers of one level of government entails a corresponding diminution in the powers of the other level of government. (This is not always the case, because the double-aspect and incidental-effect doctrines tolerate some degree of overlapping of even exclusive powers.) Subsection (4) would be an obstacle to the use of s. 2 to augment an exclusive legislative power, because it would be arguable that this constituted a derogation from the exclusive powers of the other level of government.

Subsection (4) would not prevent an increase in legislative powers that did not derogate from the powers of the other level of government, for example, an increase in powers at the expense of Charter rights. Subsection (4) protects only the powers of governmental institutions, not the rights of private individuals. So subsection (4) is irrelevant to the question of the impact of the new s. 2 on the Charter of Rights. That is the topic of the next section of this chapter.

Charter of Rights

The new s. 2 does not override the Charter of Rights. On the contrary, s. 2, as a merely interpretative provision, is subordinate to the Charter of Rights. A law passed to preserve linguistic duality or to promote the distinct identity of Quebec would, like any other law, have to comply with the Charter. If the law was contrary to the Charter of Rights, then the law would be invalid.

There are some provisions in the Constitution of Canada that do, in effect, constitute exceptions to the Charter of Rights. The provision for mandatory retirement of judges at age 75 (s. 99) is an example: the removal of a judge at age 75 could not be attacked as discrimination on the basis of age. The provision for legislation in relation to "Indians, and lands reserved for the Indians" (s. 91(24)) is another: a law relating to Indians could not be attacked as discrimination on the basis of race: *A.-G. Can. v. Canard* [1976] 1 S.C.R. 170. The provision for legislation in relation to denominational schools (s. 93(3)) is another: a denominational school law could not be attacked as discrimination on the basis of religion: *Re Bill 30 (Ontario Separate School Funding Reference)* [1987] __ S.C.R. ____. In these cases, a distinction (age, race, religion) is inevitably involved in the exercise of the power. The Charter does not render unconstitutional a distinction that is expressly permitted by another part of the Constitution. A more generally worded power, which is not inherently discriminatory, must be exercised in compliance with the Charter of Rights. Even if the linguistic dualism and distinct society clauses were grants of power (which they are not), they are not grants that are inherently discriminatory or otherwise in opposition to any Charter right, and therefore they would have to be exercised in compliance with the Charter.

A law that is inconsistent with a Charter right may be saved by s. 1 of the Charter. If the law is held to be within s. 1's phrase "such reasonable limits prescribed by law as can be demonstrably justified in a free and democratic society", then the law will be upheld. In deciding this question, the purpose of the law is one of the matters that is brought into account. The preservation of linguistic duality or the promotion of Quebec's distinct identity would undoubtedly serve as purposes that could help to characterize a law as justified under s. 1. Such purposes would qualify now, without the new s. 2. However, the new s. 2 will give those purposes some added weight. In that indirect fashion, the new s. 2 could expand the power of the Parliament or a Legislature to derogate from the Charter.

Of course, no legislative purpose, no matter how legitimate, provides automatic s. 1 justification. In *R. v. Oakes* [1986] 1 S.C.R. 103, the Supreme Court of Canada emphasized that a "proportionality test" had to be satisfied as well. The proportionality test requires the Court to be satisfied that the law impairs the guaranteed right as little as possible (least drastic means). The proportionality test also requires the Court to balance the injury to a guaranteed civil liberty against the legislative purpose. The *Oakes* test inevitably involves a policy choice by the Court, which cannot be wholly predictable, but the general thrust of the Court's ruling is to give priority to the guaranteed rights and reduce the scope of the s. 1 justification.

Clause 16 of the schedule to the Accord provides that nothing in the new s. 2 affects ss. 25 or 27 of the Charter of Rights, s. 35 of the Constitution Act, 1982 or s. 91(24) of the Constitution Act, 1867. These references are to the provisions of the Constitution dealing with aboriginal rights and multiculturalism. Clause 16 is a cautionary provision designed to reassure native people and other ethnic, linguistic or cultural communities that the recognition of linguistic duality and Quebec's distinct society is not inconsistent with the protection of other distinct communities in Canada. This conclusion could as easily be drawn from s. 2 itself, which does not imply that linguistic dualism and Quebec's distinct society are the only fundamental characteristics of Canada, and which as an interpretation clause does not in any case override other parts of the Constitution.

5

SENATE

Text of s. 25

Clause 2 of the schedule to the Meech Lake Constitutional Accord will add a new s. 25 to the Constitution Act, 1867. (The original s. 25 was repealed in 1893.) The new s. 25 provides as follows:

Names to be submitted

25. (1) Where a vacancy occurs in the Senate, the government of the province to which the vacancy relates may, in relation to that vacancy, submit to the Queen's Privy Council for Canada the names of persons who may be summoned to the Senate.

Choice of Senators from names submitted

(2) Until an amendment to the Constitution of Canada is made in relation to the Senate pursuant to section 41 of the *Constitution Act, 1982*, the person summoned to fill a vacancy in the Senate shall be chosen from among persons whose names have been submitted under subsection (1) by the government of the province to which the vacancy relates and must be acceptable to the Queen's Privy Council for Canada.

This part of the Accord is discussed in the *Report* of the Special Joint Committee on the 1987 Constitutional Accord (1987), ch. IX.

Purpose of s. 25

Senate reform was not one of Quebec's five conditions for adherence to the Constitution Act, 1982. It was dealt with in the Accord because it has traditionally been a priority item for British Columbia and Alberta, whose Premiers were reluctant to enter into a constitutional agreement that made no reference to Senate reform. The solution was to agree to provincial nominations for Senate appointments as an interim measure only, and to place Senate reform on the agenda for the next round of constitutional discussions. From the point of view of the provincial proponents of a more effective Senate, the new s. 25 constitutes an immediate improvement in the structure of the Senate, and it supplies an earnest that the federal government at least will not lose interest in the project of Senate reform.

The ultimate goal of British Columbia and Alberta is a constitutional amendment providing for a restructured Senate that would better represent regional interests in the federal Parliament. A proposal that is being promoted in western Canada is for a "Triple E Senate", that is, a Senate that is elected, equal and effective. Such a Senate would be elected directly by the people; each province would be represented by an equal number of senators; and the Senate would have effective powers. It remains to be seen whether the first ministers can reach agreement on such a body, and, if so, how it could be reconciled with an elected House of Commons to which the federal cabinet is responsible. If agreement is not reached on Senate reform, then of course the new s. 25 will remain in place. The new s. 25, although intended to be temporary, is not drafted as a temporary measure, and could therefore turn out to be permanent.

Appointments to Senate

The new s. 25 requires that appointments to the Senate be made from names submitted by the provinces. The present position under the Constitution Act, 1867 is that appointments to the Senate are made by the Governor General (s. 24), acting solely on the advice of the federal cabinet. The new s. 25 does not change the formal appointing power, and indeed by subsection (2) it is stipulated that any appointment "must be acceptable to the Queen's Privy Council for Canada" (that is, acceptable to the federal cabinet). However, under the new s. 25 the Governor General will be confined to names submitted by the provinces.

Sections 21 and 22 of the Constitution Act, 1867 prescribe the numbers and the distribution of senators. Distribution is premised on a division of Canada into four regions, each with an equal number of senators. The four regions are (1) Ontario, (2) Quebec, (3) the three maritime provinces, and (4) the four western provinces. Each region has 24 senators. In addition, when Newfoundland joined Canada in 1949 it was given six senators; and in 1975 the two territories were each given one senator. The total membership of the Senate is therefore 104 members, and the provincial and territorial representation is as follows:

Ontario	24
Quebec	24
Nova Scotia	10
New Brunswick	10
Prince Edward Island	4
Manitoba	6

British Columbia	6
Saskatchewan	6
Alberta	6
Newfoundland	6
Yukon Territory	1
Northwest Territories	1
	104

When a senator dies or retires, the vacancy must be filled by a new senator who is resident in the province to which the vacancy relates. Before the Meech Lake Constitutional Accord, the person was chosen by the federal government without any obligation to consider the wishes of the provincial government. The Accord requires all future appointments to be made from names submitted by the provincial government. Moreover, it will be recalled that the Meech Lake political accord requires this mode of appointment to start immediately, even before the Accord is ratified and proclaimed into force.

The new s. 25 (and the political accord) requires a Senate vacancy to be filled from names submitted by "the government of *the province* to which the vacancy relates" (my emphasis). This language is not apt to cover vacancies in the two Senate seats from the territories. Presumably, these two seats will continue to be filled with people of the federal government's own choice, as was the case before the Meech Lake Constitutional Accord. (*Report* of Special Joint Committee on the 1987 Constitutional Accord (1987), 90.)

The new s. 25 is silent as to how the government of each province is to select the names for submission to the federal government. That will be for each provincial government to decide for itself. Most likely, a government will select members of its political party as an act of patronage. It is possible, however, that a provincial government could organize an election for the purpose of yielding a name to fill a vacancy.

Senate reform

As noted earlier, the new s. 25 is not intended to be a permanent feature of the Constitution. It is intended to serve as a transitional measure until a more thoroughgoing reform of the Senate is undertaken. This is contemplated by clause 13 of the Meech Lake Constitutional Accord, which inserts a new s. 50 into the Constitution Act, 1982. The new s. 50 calls for a constitutional conference of first ministers no later than 1988, and at least annually thereafter, to consider (among other things):

> Senate reform, including the role and functions of the Senate, its powers, the method of selecting Senators and representation in the Senate.

When Senate reform is embarked upon at a future constitutional conference, any resulting agreement will have to be unanimous. Clause 9 of the Meech Lake Constitutional Accord makes some changes in the constitutional amending procedures. These are discussed in chapter 9 of this volume (Amending Formula). One of these changes is to require the "unanimity" amending procedure of s. 41 for amendments relating to "the powers of the Senate and the method of selecting Senators", and "the number of members by which a province is entitled to be represented in the Senate and the residence qualifications of Senators". At present, these topics are covered by the amending procedure of s. 42, which requires the assent of the Senate and House of Commons and only two-thirds of the provinces representing 50 per cent of the population. The Meech Lake Accord's requirement of unanimity works at cross purposes to the other provisions regarding the Senate, because the change in the amending formula will make Senate reform more difficult to achieve. However, there is force to the argument that a change to a Triple E Senate, or some variant of that, is too important to be thrust upon an unwilling province. On that view, unanimity is a wise safeguard.

There is obviously a real possibility that in future rounds of constitutional discussions the first ministers will fail to reach agreement on Senate reform. If that happened, then the new s. 25 would become permanent. As senators retired or died, the Senate might gradually evolve into a "house of the provinces" with its members feeling themselves primarily beholden to their province of origin rather than to any federal political party. This would probably change the character of the institution, making it more assertive in representing provincial or regional interests. At present, although the Senate was originally conceived as a protector of regional interests, it has not functioned in that way, and the main reason is that its members are appointed solely by the federal government. By removing this fatal flaw in the constitution of the Senate, s. 25 could turn out to be one of the most significant of the changes agreed to at Meech Lake. This would be an ironic result since Senate reform was not part of the agenda of the Quebec round of constitutional discussions that led up to Meech Lake.

6

IMMIGRATION

Text of ss. 95A to 95E

Clause 3 of the schedule to the Meech Lake Constitutional Accord will insert five new sections after s. 95 of the Constitution Act, 1867. The new ss. 95A to 95E provide as follows:

Agreements on Immigration and Aliens

Commitment to negotiate

95A. The Government of Canada shall, at the request of the government of any province, negotiate with the government of that province for the purpose of concluding an agreement relating to immigration or the temporary admission of aliens into that province that is appropriate to the needs and circumstances of that province.

Agreements

95B. (1) Any agreement concluded between Canada and a province in relation to immigration or the temporary admission of aliens into that province has the force of law from the time it is declared to do so in accordance with subsection 95C(1) and shall from that time have effect notwithstanding class 25 of section 91 or section 95.

Limitation

(2) An agreement that has the force of law under subsection (1) shall have effect only so long and so far as it is not repugnant to any provision of an Act of the Parliament of Canada that sets national standards and objectives relating to immigration or aliens, including any provision that establishes general classes of immigrants or relates to levels of immigration for Canada or that prescribes classes of individuals who are inadmissible into Canada.

Application of Charter

(3) The *Canadian Charter of Rights and Freedoms* applies in respect of any agreement that has the force of law under subsection (1) and in respect of anything done by the Parliament or Government of Canada, or the legislature or government of a province, pursuant to any such agreement.

Proclamation relating to agreements

95C. (1) A declaration that an agreement referred to in subsection 95B(1) has the force of law may be made by proclamation issued by the Governor General under the Great Seal of Canada only where so authorized by resolutions of the Senate and House of Commons and of the legislative assembly of the province that is a party to the agreement.

Amendment of agreements

(2) An amendment to an agreement referred to in subsection 95B(1) may be made by proclamation issued by the Governor General under the Great Seal of Canada only where so authorized

(a) by resolutions of the Senate and House of Commons and of the legislative assembly of the province that is a party to the agreement; or

(b) in such other manner as is set out in the agreement.

Application of sections 46 to 48 of *Constitution Act, 1982*

95D. Sections 46 to 48 of the *Constitution Act, 1982* apply, with such modifications as the circumstances require, in respect of any declaration made pursuant to subsection 95C(1), any amendment to an agreement made pursuant to subsection 95C(2) or any amendment made pursuant to section 95E.

Amendments to sections 95A to 95D or this section

95E. An amendment to sections 95A to 95D or this section may be made in accordance with the procedure set out in subsection 38(1) of the *Constitution Act, 1982*, but only if the amendment is authorized by resolutions of the legislative assemblies of all the provinces that are, at the time of the amendment, parties to an agreement that has the force of law under subsection 95B(1).

This part of the Accord is discussed in the *Report* of the Special Joint Committee on the 1987 Constitutional Accord (1987), ch. X.

Purpose of ss. 95A to 95E

The new ss. 95A to 95E provide a mechanism for the establishment of defined roles for the two levels of government in the field of immigration.

The present constitutional position is contained in s. 95 of the Constitution Act, 1867. Section 95 grants to the federal Parliament and the provincial Legislatures concurrent powers over immigration. Federal paramountcy is retained by a provision that requires provincial law to yield to federal law where the provincial law is "repugnant to" (inconsistent with) the federal law. This provision deals with conflict between federal and provincial law, but s. 95 nowhere indicates in what fashion the concurrent powers are to be shared.

Quebec has always been more concerned than the other provinces about the size and composition of its immigrant groups, and especially their ability to settle in a predominantly French-speaking environment. Since 1971, immigration to the province of Quebec has been governed by a series of agreements between the federal and Quebec governments, of which the current version is the Cullen-Couture agreement of 1979. The main purpose of these agreements is to enable Quebec to participate in the selection of persons who wish to settle permanently or temporarily in Quebec. (The way in which the Cullen-Couture agreement works is described in the *Report* of the Special Joint Committee on the 1987 Constitutional Accord (1987), 101-103). Six of the other provinces have also entered into similar agreements with the federal government (*Report*, above, 98). British Columbia, Manitoba and Ontario have not entered into agreements.

The new ss. 95A to 95E make constitutional provision for immigration agreements between Canada and the provinces. Section 95A imposes on the government of Canada an obligation to negotiate with a province that wishes to conclude an immigration agreement. Sections 95B to 95E then confer a constitutional status on any agreement that is successfully concluded and implemented in accordance with the procedures established by those sections.

The new ss. 95A to 95E are supplemented by the Meech Lake political accord that was described earlier in chapter 3, Political Accord. The political accord, by clause 2, includes an undertaking by the federal government to conclude an immigration agreement with Quebec that would incorporate many of the principles of the existing Cullen-Couture agreement; that would guarantee Quebec a proportionate share in the annual national quota of immigrants; and that would transfer some settlement functions from Canada to Quebec. What is contemplated, obviously, is that the negotiation of this agreement should proceed forthwith, so that an agreement could be in place when the Meech Lake constitutional amendments come into force, which will enable the agreement to be entrenched without unnecessary delay. The political accord, by clause 4, also contemplates the negotiation of similar agreements with other provinces.

Constitutional status of agreements

The existing federal-provincial immigration agreements are authorized by the federal Immigration Act, 1976, S.C. 1976-77, c. 52, s. 109(2). They do not have constitutional status, and could therefore be abrogated or altered by a federal statute. The contribution of the new ss. 95A to 95E is to make it possible to confer a degree of constitutional protection on an immigration agreement so as to shield it from the unilateral legislative power of the federal Parliament. The shield is not complete: as will be explained later in this chapter, by virtue of s. 95B(2), Parliament retains the power to set "national standards and objectives relating to immigration or aliens".

Section 95C provides the procedure to "constitutionalize" a federal-provincial immigration agreement. The agreement must be ratified by resolutions of the Senate and House of Commons and of the legislative assembly of the province that is a party to the agreement; then the agreement must be proclaimed in force by the Governor General. This is the same procedure as is stipulated by s. 43 of the Constitution Act, 1982 for an amendment to any provision of the Constitution of Canada that applies to one or more, but not all, provinces. Once an agreement has been entrenched in this fashion, it can be amended only by the same procedure, unless the agreement itself makes a different provision for its own amendment. Section 94D makes certain machinery provisions of the constitutional amending procedures (ss. 46 to 48) applicable to agreements and amendments of agreements. Section 94E provides that any amendments of ss. 95A to 95E themselves must include approvals by all the provinces that are parties to entrenched immigration agreements.

Federal legislative power

The main purpose of ss. 95A to 95E is, as noted earlier, to place federal-provincial immigration agreements beyond the reach of unilateral federal legislative power. That purpose is articulated by subsection (1) of s. 95B, which establishes the general rule that an agreement takes priority over federal legislative power over immigration (s. 95) and naturalization and aliens (s. 91(25)). However, subsection (2) of s. 95B carves out an important exception to the general rule. Subsection (2) preserves the power of the federal Parliament to set "national standards and objectives relating to immigration or aliens". A federal law that is characterized as setting "national standards and objectives" thus remains competent to the federal Parliament, and will be paramount over any inconsistent terms of an immigration agreement. A federal law that is not characterized as setting national standards and objectives will be ineffective in the face of any inconsistent terms of an immigration agreement. The phrase "national standards and objectives" thus marks a crucial boundary line. It is not exhaustively defined, and is obviously far from clear. However, subsection (2) of s. 95B removes some kinds of laws from the realm of dispute by specifically providing that the phrase includes "any provision that establishes general classes of immigrants or relates to levels of immigration for Canada or that prescribes classes of individuals who are inadmissible into Canada".

The reservation of federal power over national standards and objectives means that the federal Parliament is not disabled from establishing new national immigration policies in response to changes in demographic needs, political values, and international obligations. Federal leadership in a matter of vital national concern would be stultified if a new immigration policy could only be implemented by the formal amendment of all federal-provincial agreements that reflected an older policy. Subsection (2) of s. 94B preserves an essential core of federal power by authorizing federal laws setting national standards and objectives, and by making such laws paramount over any conflicting provision of a federal-provincial agreement.

Mobility of immigrants

The Charter of Rights is not overriden by an immigration agreement, even after the agreement has been constitutionalized. Subsection (3) of s. 95B makes clear that the Charter continues to apply. Thus, immigrants entering Canada will enjoy the rights conferred by the Charter. These rights include the mobility rights of s. 6. For example, an immigrant to Quebec, who has been selected as part of Quebec's quota in accordance with the provisions of an immigration agreement, is not bound to remain in Quebec. In practice, he or she is free to move to another part of Canada, and if the immigrant "has the status of a permanent resident" that freedom is constitutionally guaranteed by s. 6.

There is a good deal of movement by immigrants from the province of reception to other parts of Canada. The Joint Committee found that more than a third of the immigrants to Quebec in recent years had moved to another province (*Report of the Special Joint Committee on the 1987 Constitutional Accord* (1987), 100). There is in fact nothing in the existing immigration agreements to prevent this, but, in the unlikely event that restrictions on post-reception mobility were introduced into new agreements, s. 6 of the Charter would prevail.

7

SUPREME COURT OF CANADA

Text of ss. 101A to 101E

Clauses 4 and 5 of the schedule to the Meech Lake Constitutional Accord will insert three new sub-headings into the Judicature part of the Constitution Act, 1867, and after s. 101 will insert five new sections. The five new sections are ss. 101A to 101E, which provide as follows:

Supreme Court of Canada

Supreme Court continued

101A. (1) The court existing under the name of the Supreme Court of Canada is hereby continued as the general court of appeal for Canada, and as an additional court for the better administration of the laws of Canada, and shall continue to be a superior court of record.

Constitution of court

(2) The Supreme Court of Canada shall consist of a chief justice to be called the Chief Justice of Canada and eight other judges, who shall be appointed by the Governor General in Council by letters patent under the Great Seal.

Who may be appointed judges

101B. (1) Any person may be appointed a judge of the Supreme Court of Canada who, after having been admitted to the bar of any province or territory, has, for a total of at least ten years, been a judge of any court in Canada or a member of the bar of any province or territory.

Three judges from Quebec

(2) At least three judges of the Supreme Court of Canada shall be appointed from among persons who, after having been admitted to the bar of Quebec,

have, for a total of at least ten years, been judges of any court of Quebec or of any court established by the Parliament of Canada, or members of the bar of Quebec.

Names may be submitted

101C. (1) Where a vacancy occurs in the Supreme Court of Canada, the government of each province may, in relation to that vacancy, submit to the Minister of Justice of Canada the names of any of the persons who have been admitted to the bar of that province and are qualified under section 101B for appointment to that court.

Appointment from names submitted

(2) Where an appointment is made to the Supreme Court of Canada, the Governor General in Council shall, except where the Chief Justice is appointed from among members of the Court, appoint a person whose name has been submitted under subsection (1) and who is acceptable to the Queen's Privy Council for Canada.

Appointment from Quebec

(3) Where an appointment is made in accordance with subsection (2) of any of the three judges necessary to meet the requirement set out in subsection 101B(2), the Governor General in Council shall appoint a person whose name has been submitted by the Government of Quebec.

Appointment from other provinces

(4) Where an appointment is made in accordance with subsection (2) otherwise than as required under subsection (3), the Governor General in Council shall appoint a person whose name has been submitted by the government of a province other than Quebec.

Tenure, salaries, etc., of judges

101D. Sections 99 and 100 apply in respect of the judges of the Supreme Court of Canada.

Relationship to section 101

101E. (1) Sections 101A to 101D shall not be construed as abrogating or derogating from the powers of the Parliament of Canada to make laws under section 101 except to the extent that such laws are inconsistent with those sections.

References to the Supreme Court of Canada

(2) For greater certainty, section 101A shall not be construed as abrogating or derogating from the powers of the Parliament of Canada to make laws relating to the reference of questions of law or fact, or any other matters, to the Supreme Court of Canada.

This part of the Accord is discussed in the *Report* of the Special Joint Committee on the 1987 Constitutional Accord (1987), ch. VIII.

Statutory basis of Court

The Supreme Court of Canada was not established by the British North America Act (Constitution Act, 1867) at the time of confederation. At that time, there was controversy over whether a final court within Canada was necessary, and the view that it was unnecessary prevailed. It must be remembered that in 1867 the Judicial Committee of the Privy Council served as a final court of appeal for all British colonies, including those of British North America, and that right of appeal continued after confederation. Indeed, that right of appeal was not finally abolished until 1949.

The Constitution Act, 1867, while not establishing a Supreme Court of Canada, did authorize its establishment at some future date. Section 101 of the Constitution Act, 1867 conferred on the federal Parliament the power to "provide for the constitution, maintenance, and organization of a general court of appeal for Canada". In 1875, the federal Parliament exercised this power and enacted a statute establishing the Supreme Court of Canada. The Act was the Supreme and Exchequer Courts Act, 1875, and it also established the Exchequer Court of Canada, which has now been replaced by the Federal Court of Canada. The current statute governing the Supreme Court of Canada is the Supreme Court Act, R.S.C. 1970, c. S-19.

The Supreme Court of Canada was thus created by an ordinary federal statute, and its existence, jurisdiction, composition and organization continue to depend upon an ordinary federal statute. Subject to the doubts expressed in the next section of this chapter, it is still the case that changes to the Court's statute can be enacted by the federal Parliament in exercise of the power conferred by s. 101 of the Constitution Act, 1867. Since 1875, many important changes to the composition, jurisdiction and procedures of the Court have been enacted by the federal Parliament. In theory, the Court could be abolished by the federal Parliament. Of course, this is not a practical possibility. Nevertheless, there is widespread agreement that the Court should be entrenched in the Constitution so as to place it outside the reach of federal legislative power. It is inappropriate that the Court which serves as the guardian of the Constitution should be unprotected by the Constitution.

Constitution Act, 1982

In the intergovernmental constitutional discussions that occurred in the 1970s, the entrenchment of the Court was one of the principal items on the agenda. However, apparently because of the difficulty of achieving agreement on some aspects, especially a provincial role in the appointment of judges, the entrenchment of the Court was not included in the constitutional proposals that were placed before the federal Parliament by Prime Minister Trudeau in October 1980, and the entrenchment of the Court was not included in the constitutional settlement that was approved by all first ministers except for the Premier of Quebec in

November 1981. The result was that the Constitution Act, 1982 did not place the Supreme Court of Canada in the Constitution of Canada.

While the Constitution Act, 1982 did not make provision for the existence of the Supreme Court of Canada, it did include two references to the Court in Part V of the Act, which provides the procedures for amending the Constitution of Canada. Section 41(d) requires that the unanimity amending procedure be used for amendments to "the composition of the Supreme Court of Canada". Section 42(1)(d) requires that the standard seven-fifty procedure (the federal government and two-thirds of the provinces representing 50 per cent of the population) be used for amendments to the Constitution relating to "the Supreme Court of Canada" (other than its "composition").

The two references to the Supreme Court of Canada in ss. 41 and 42 of the Constitution Act, 1982 are puzzling. On a literal reading of ss. 41 and 42, they seem to be completely ineffective. Sections 41 and 42 apply only to amendments to the "Constitution of Canada". The Constitution of Canada is a term that is defined in s. 52(2) of the Constitution Act, 1982, and the list of instruments that are included does not include the Supreme Court Act. It would seem to follow that the federal Parliament is still free to amend the Supreme Court Act by enacting a statute in exercise of its power under s. 101 of the Constitution Act, 1867. This is evidently the legal advice that has been provided to the present federal government, because it has introduced a bill to amend the Supreme Court Act by permitting the disposition of applications for leave without oral argument, and by authorizing the delivery of judgments otherwise than in open court: Bill C-53, first reading, May 4, 1987.

Some constitutional scholars, troubled by the conclusion that ss. 41(d) and 42(1)(d) have no work to do, have argued that these provisions have accomplished the entrenchment of the Court. According to this view, ss. 41(d) and 42(1)(d) have, by implication, made the Supreme Court Act part of the Constitution of Canada, and changes to the Court must now follow the amending procedures of ss. 41 and 42. This is the view of Professor R.I. Cheffins, "The Constitution Act, 1982 and the Amending Formula" (1982) 4 Supreme Court L.R. 42. It is also the view of Professor W.R. Lederman, "Constitutional Procedure and the Reform of the Supreme Court of Canada" (1985) 26 Cahiers de droit 195, who suggests, however, that only those parts of the Supreme Court Act defining the "basic elements" of the Court are part of the Constitution of Canada; the rest can be amended by the Parliament of Canada under s. 101.

The references to the Supreme Court of Canada in ss. 41(d) and 42(1)(d) of the Constitution Act, 1982 have created an intolerably confusing situation. While it is probable that these references are ineffective as long as the Court is not provided for in the Constitution of Canada, this is by no means clear; and it is possible that the Supreme Court Act, or some as yet unidentified parts of the Supreme Court Act, cannot now be amended by the ordinary legislative process. The situation cries out for clarification, and clarification has now been provided by the Meech Lake Constitutional Accord.

Entrenchment of Court

The new ss. 101A to 101E that are proposed by the Meech Lake Constitutional Accord make explicit provision for the Supreme Court of Canada in the Constitution of Canada. The new s. 41(g) of the Constitution Act, 1982, which is also proposed by the Meech Lake Constitutional Accord, and which is discussed in chapter 9, Amending Formula, below, now requires the unanimity amending procedure for an amendment to the Constitution of Canada in relation to "the Supreme Court of Canada". It is now perfectly plain that the existence and principal characteristics of the Court are entrenched in the Constitution beyond the reach of the unilateral legislative power of the federal Parliament.

It is also plain that the unanimity amending procedure is applicable only to changes in the constitutional text. Section 101E places this beyond doubt by providing that the new constitutional provisions do not derogate from the power of the federal Parliament to make laws under s. 101 except to the extent that such laws are inconsistent with the new constitutional provisions. In other words, those aspects of the Court that are not provided for in ss. 101A to 101D are still open to change by the unilateral action of the federal Parliament, or by rules and regulations made under the authority of the federal Parliament.

Jurisdiction of Court

The new s. 101A(1) describes the Court as a "general court of appeal for Canada", and as "an additional court for the better administration of the laws of Canada". These are phrases that are now in s. 101 of the Constitution Act, 1867, and it is appropriate that there should be no confusing divergence between s. 101 and the new text. The phrase "general court of appeal for Canada" covers the Court's appellate jurisdiction. The phrase "additional court for the better administration of the laws of Canada" makes clear that the Court can also be given original jurisdiction by federal law. In fact, the Court has been given very little original jurisdiction. (In *Gulf Oil Corp. v. Gulf Canada* [1980] 2 S.C.R. 39, the Court held that the Canada Evidence Act conferred on the Court an original jurisdiction to issue letters rogatory.)

The Court does possess a kind of original jurisdiction in its reference jurisdiction, under which the Court answers questions referred to it by the federal government: Supreme Court Act, s. 55(1). Because the answers to reference questions do not dispose of actual controversies and are merely advisory, the Court's reference jurisdiction is not a truly judicial function. The anomalous character of the Court's reference jurisdiction is acknowledged by new s. 101E(2), which provides that ss. 101A to 101D are not to be construed as taking away the power of the federal Parliament to confer the reference jurisdiction on the Court. The purpose of s. 101E(2) is to make clear that the definition of the Court's jurisdiction in new s. 101A is not to be held to exclude the non-judicial function of rendering advisory opinions. In other words, the Privy Council decision that upheld the reference jurisdiction in 1912 (*A.-G. Ont. v. A.-G. Can.* (Reference Appeal) [1912] A.C. 571) is still good law, despite the entrenchment of the Court and its jurisdiction.

New s. 101A does not go beyond the general phrases of s. 101 in articulating the jurisdiction of the Court. The text says nothing more specific about the jurisdiction of the Court, leaving the details to federal legislative power under s. 101. That is important to preserve flexibility with respect to changes in the Court's jurisdiction that will in the future, as in the past, turn out to be desirable. This would not give to the federal Parliament the power to reduce the Court to insignificance through reductions in its jurisdiction, because any change in the Court's jurisdiction would have to be compatible with the description "a general court of appeal for Canada", and the implications of that phrase, like any other constitutional question, would ultimately be decided by the Court itself.

Composition of Court

The new s. 101(A)(2) provides that the Court shall consist of a Chief Justice and eight other judges. This is the existing position of course. After it has been entrenched in the Constitution, any future change in the number of judges will be able to be accomplished only by the unanimity amending procedure of s. 41.

A committee of the Canadian Bar Association has criticized the entrenchment of the number of judges on the Court, arguing that it would be preferable not to stipulate a particular number, so that the size of the Court can be adjusted from time to time by the federal Parliament. The Committee pointed out that the size of the Court has been changed three times in the past, and that changes will probably be desired in the future. (*Report* of the Canadian Bar Association Committee on the Supreme Court of Canada (1987), 18). On the other hand, as the Committee recognized, it could be argued that the number of judges ought to be entrenched to avoid any possibility of court-packing by the federal Parliament, as was attempted in the United States by President Roosevelt in the 1930s to overcome decisions adverse to his New Deal program. From this standpoint, entrenchment of the number of judges becomes one of the guarantees of the independence of the Court. Of course, the new requirement of provincial nomination of judges is also a safeguard against the federal government packing the Court.

Regional representation of judges

The new s. 101B(2) provides that "at least three" of the nine judges must be appointed from the bench or bar of Quebec. This provision constitutionalizes the status quo: s. 6 of the Supreme Court Act makes the same stipulation.

The statutory requirement — soon to be a constitutional requirement — that at least three of the nine judges be drawn from Quebec is supplemented by conventional understandings that three judges should come from Ontario, one from the four Atlantic provinces and two from the four western provinces. The Chief Justice has always been appointed from the existing judges, and the appointment has usually alternated between French-speaking and English-speaking incumbents. (The practice of alternation has occasionally been departed from, most recently by the appointment of Dickson C.J. to succeed Laskin C.J.).

The nature of the judicial function, as understood in Canada and other countries in which the judiciary is independent, does not allow a judge to "represent" the region from which he or she was appointed in any direct sense, and certainly does not allow the judge to favour the arguments of persons or governments from that region. What regional representation is supposed to do, however, is to ensure that there are judges on the Court who are personally familiar with each major region of the country, and who can bring to the decision of a case from that region an understanding of that region's distinctive legal, social and economic character.

With respect to Quebec, the statutory requirement of three judges is of particular importance. The distinct cultural and linguistic make-up of Quebec, and in particular its system of civil law, make it imperative that there be a core of Quebeckers on the Court. Only the Quebec judges are likely to have been trained in and to have practised the civil law, and only the Quebec judges are likely to have practised law in the French language. Their presence is therefore important for cases raising issues of civil law and for cases argued in the French language.

Appointment of judges

The new s. 101A(2) provides that the judges of the Court are to be appointed by the Governor General in Council. This power is subject to the new s. 101C, which requires the Governor in Council to appoint a person whose name has been submitted by the government of a province and who is also acceptable to the federal government. Thus, when one of the three judges from Quebec dies or retires, the vacancy must be filled from Quebec by a person who is acceptable to both the government of Quebec and the government of Canada. When one of the three judges from Ontario dies or retires, fidelity to past practice would require that the vacancy be filled from Ontario by a person who is acceptable to both the government of Ontario and the government of Canada. For the remaining three positions on the Court, the conventional distribution is by region rather than province, so that the federal government could examine names submitted by several western provinces before selecting one to fill a western vacancy, and a similar choice would be open in filling an Atlantic vacancy.

The new s. 101C contains no mechanism for breaking a deadlock. What is to happen if the federal government finds none of the names submitted by a province acceptable? This does not seem to be a realistic concern where the vacancy to be filled is from outside Quebec. If the federal government finds one province's list of names to be unacceptable, it can consider the list of another province. This is even true when the vacancy is from Ontario, because Ontario's informal quota of three judges is not a hard-and-fast rule. It has, in fact, been departed from once: in 1978, when McIntyre J. from British Columbia replaced Spence J. from Ontario. (Ontario's quota was restored in 1982, when Wilson J. from Ontario replaced Martland J. from Alberta.) However, when the vacancy to be filled is one of Quebec's constitutionally-guaranteed quota of three places, there is no escape from the requirement that the governments of Quebec and Canada must reach agreement on a candidate. In the event that agreement could not be reached, no appointment could be made, and the Court would have to function with only eight members and with only two Quebeckers until the political situation changed so as to enable the deadlock to be broken.

The new s. 101C has the effect of excluding from appointment lawyers from the two territories. Section 101B expressly allows membership of the bar of a territory as a qualification for appointment. But s. 101C makes no provision for the submission of names by the governments of the territories (as opposed to the provinces), and no name can be submitted by a provincial government of a person who has not been a member of the bar of that province. Thus, s. 101C effectively precludes the name of a person practising in the territories from getting onto a list of candidates for appointment. The probable reason for this oversight is that appointments have in the past usually been made of persons who have practised in the larger urban centres, and no one has ever been appointed from the territories. Also, the informal regional "quotas" that were earlier described are always expressed in terms of provinces: they do not contemplate that a judge could be drawn from the territories. Nonetheless, the Joint Committee took the view that the Constitution should not preclude the appointment of a qualified person from the territories. The Joint Committee accordingly recommended that s. 101C be amended to enable the territorial governments to submit names for appointment. (*Report* of the Special Joint Committee on the 1987 Constitutional Accord (1987), 87.)

The new procedure for the appointment of judges is the only substantive change in the Supreme Court of Canada that is made by the Meech Lake Constitutional Accord. The new procedure gives to the provinces a direct role in the appointing process by requiring that each appointment to the Court be agreeable to the government of the province from which the appointment is made.

The present position, which is provided for in s. 4 of the Supreme Court Act, is that appointments to the Court are made by the Governor in Council, which means, of course, the federal cabinet. There is no provision for provincial involvement in the selection process, and this has been a longstanding grievance by some provincial governments, especially those of Quebec and the western provinces. Their argument is that the Court has to serve as umpire of federal-provincial disputes about the interpretation of the Constitution, and it is not appropriate that the judges be appointed by only one side to the dispute. The force of this argument has been widely recognized for a long time, but until Meech Lake a suitable formula for sharing the appointing power has always eluded the first ministers.

The Meech Lake amendments meet the criticism that the provinces ought to play a role in the selection of judges of the Supreme Court of Canada. They do not meet a different criticism, which is that the appointing process ought to be more open and better informed by the views of people outside the cabinets of the federal and (now) provincial governments. Two committees of the Canadian Bar Association and one committee of the Canadian Association of Law Teachers have recommended that the names of candidates for appointment should be generated by a well-informed advisory committee, which could include representatives of the bench, bar, both levels of government and non-lawyers. Such a committee could be established in each province to suggest the names that the province would submit to the federal government for consideration for appointment. (Report of the Canadian Association of Law Teachers Special Committee on the Appointment of Judges (1985); Report of the Canadian Bar Association Committee on the Appointment of Judges in Canada (1985), 66-68; Report of the Canadian Bar Association Committee on the Supreme Court of Canada (1987), 49.) There is, of course, no need for such a committee to be provided for in the Constitution, or even in a statute. Its establishment and role could be quite informal.

The Meech Lake amendments, even if not supplemented by provincial advisory committees of the kind suggested by the Bar and Law Teachers, should have no adverse effect on the quality of appointments to the Court. The high reputation of the Court has caused successive federal governments to appoint only well qualified people to the Court. I see no reason to suppose that approval by two governments rather than one would lead to any change in this admirable practice. Indeed, for appointments from outside Quebec, the federal government is in a position to shop around among provincial lists, which should create a healthy competition among the provinces to produce the most highly qualified candidate.

Tenure of judges

The new s. 101D provides that ss. 99 and 100 of the Constitution Act, 1867 apply in respect of the judges of the Supreme Court of Canada.

Section 99 of the Constitution Act, 1867 guarantees the tenure of the judges of the superior courts of the provinces "during good behaviour". This rather quaint language comes from the Act of Settlement, 1701(U.K.), which has always been treated as a guarantee of the independence of the judiciary. (Section 99, as amended in1960, also provides for mandatory retirement of judges at age 75.) Section 100 of the Constitution Act, 1867 provides that the salaries of the judges of the superior, district and county courts of the provinces shall be "fixed and provided by the Parliament of Canada". This provision is also a safeguard of judicial independence in that it requires salaries to be fixed by Parliament, thereby precluding executive interference with the remuneration of the judges.

Sections 99 and 100 do not now apply to the judges of the Supreme Court of Canada. It is an anomaly that the judges of the Supreme Court of Canada do not enjoy the same level of constitutional protection of their independence as is possessed by the judges of the higher provincial courts. The new s. 101D, by aplying ss. 99 and 100 to the judges of the Supreme Court of Canada, removes that anomaly.

The Meech Lake amendments support judicial independence in another way as well. By entrenching the existence and essential features of the Court in the Constitution, ss. 101A to 101E place the Court as an institution out of the reach of federal legislative power. In practice, this step is no doubt unnecessary, because the federal Parliament is unlikely ever to contemplate the abolition or diminution of the Court. In theory, however, it seems wrong that the Court, which has to serve as the neutral adjudicator of federal-provincial disputes, should be subject to the legislative power of one of the governments. For this — admittedly only symbolic — reason, it is generally agreed that the Court should be accorded the same constitutional status as the Supreme Court of the United States and the High Court of Australia: the Court should be provided for in the Constitution. This is accomplished by the Meech Lake amendments.

8

SPENDING PROVISION

Text of s. 106A

Clause 7 of the Meech Lake Constitutional Accord will add a new s. 106A to the Constitution Act, 1867. The new s. 106A provides as follows:

106A. (1) The Government of Canada shall provide reasonable compensation to the government of a province that chooses not to participate in a national shared-cost program that is established by the Government of Canada after the coming into force of this section in an area of exclusive provincial jurisdiction, if the province carries on a program or initiative that is compatible with the national objectives.

(2) Nothing in this section extends the legislative powers of the Parliament of Canada or of the legislatures of the provinces.

This part of the Accord is discussed in the *Report* of the Special Joint Committee on the 1987 Constitutional Accord (1987), ch. VII.

Purpose of s. 106A

The purpose of the new s. 106A is to limit the spending power of the federal Parliament. If the spending power is used to establish a national shared-cost program in an area of exclusive provincial jurisdiction, s. 106A requires, in effect, that any such program must include an opting-out alternative for any province that chooses not to participate in the national program. Any province that chooses to opt-out must receive "reasonable compensation" from the government of Canada, provided that the province carries on "a program or initiative that is compatible with the national objectives". This is a change in the present constitutional position, which is that the federal Parliament need not compensate provinces that choose not to participate in a national shared-cost program.

Background to s. 106A

The Parliament of Canada has the power to spend the money that it raises through taxes, borrowing, and other means. Curiously, this "spending power" is nowhere explicit in the Constitution Act, 1867, but must be inferred from some or all of the powers to legislate for the peace, order, and good government of Canada (s. 91 opening words), to levy taxes (s. 91(3)), to legislate in relation to "public property" (s. 91(1A)), and to appropriate federal funds (s. 106). An account of the existing law is to be found in Hogg, *Constitutional Law of Canada* (2nd ed., 1985), 123-126.

The federal spending power is the basis for the establishment by the government of Canada of national shared-cost programs. These programs are designed and established by the government of Canada, but are only partially funded by that government. The federal contribution to the funding of the program in a particular province is made conditional upon the provincial government contributing a share of the cost. The largest of the shared-cost programs is the health care program. This was initially established as two separate programs, one for hospital services which came into force in 1958, and the other for physicians' services which came into force in 1968. Now both programs have been amalgamated by the Canada Health Act, S.C. 1983-84, c. 6. Under this Act, the federal government makes contributions to provincial health care plans, which are plans covering the provision of hospital and physician services. The provincial health care plans are each established by provincial legislation, medical services being a provincial responsibility. However, the Canada Health Act stipulates conditions for a province to qualify for a full federal cash contribution to its health care insurance plan. The province's plan must satisfy criteria coming under five heads, namely, (1) public administration, (2) comprehensiveness, (3) universality, (4) portability, and (5) accessibility. Under the last head there is the controversial ban on extra-billing by doctors. If a provincial health care plan does not satisfy the federal conditions, the Act makes provision for the withholding or reduction of the federal cash contribution.

Provincial participation in a national shared-cost program is voluntary. In practice, however, there is substantial pressure to participate, because a refusal to participate would deny to the province the federal grant that represents the federal contribution to the program. Once a province decides to participate, it is committed to the funding of a program that the province neither designed nor established. Many of the programs, and the health care program is again the most important example, are within provincial legislative jurisdiction, and require provincial legislation for their implementation. The national shared-cost programs thus exercise a heavy influence on provincial spending and legislative priorities.

In 1969, the federal government issued a white paper that acknowledged criticism by the provinces to the effect that federal shared-cost programs forced upon the provinces changes in their priorities. The white paper suggested that, in future, shared-cost programs should be subject to two requirements: (1) a program within provincial jurisdiction should not be established until there existed "a broad national consensus in favour of the programme", and (2) each province should have the right to participate in the programme without "fiscal penalty". (Trudeau, *Federal-Provincial Grants and the Spending Power of Parliament* (1969), 36.) While the federal government never publicly adopted these two principles as its policy, they probably did become federal policy. Since 1969, no new programs have been established, and there has never been any public suggestion of a program that would violate the principles of the 1969 white paper. At the very least, the federal government would be subject to intense political pressure to structure any new shared-cost program in such a way that a province could opt out of the program without fiscal penalty.

The new s. 106A will constitutionalize the principle that a province may opt out of a shared-cost program without fiscal penalty. Section 106A will impose on the federal government a constitutional obligation to provide "reasonable compensation" to the government of a province that chooses not to participate in a national shared-cost program in an area of exclusive provincial jurisdiction, provided that the province carries on a program that is "compatible with the national objectives". Section 106A thus requires the federal government to respect provincial autonomy when it develops federal policies in areas of provincial jurisdiction.

Clarification of federal power

The explanatory commentary to the Meech Lake Constitutional Accord, issued by the federal government, says that the purpose of s. 106A "is not to define or extend the spending power of Parliament". (*A Guide to the Meech Lake Constitutional Accord*, Government of Canada, 1987, p. 6.) Nevertheless, s. 106A assumes that the federal Parliament possesses the power to establish and fund a "shared-cost program" in an area of "exclusive provincial jurisdiction". It also assumes that the federal Parliament can attach conditions to its grants to the provinces, because it assumes the existence of a "national shared-cost program", and cost-sharing contemplates, I think, grants that are conditional at least in the sense that (1) they must be applied by the province to the shared-cost program, and (2) they must be matched by some level of provincial contribution. Finally, s. 106A assumes that there can be "national objectives" in an area of exclusive provincial jurisdiction. In my view, all of these propositions accurately state the present constitutional law: Hogg, *Constitutional Law of Canada* (2nd ed., 1987), 123-126. But the present law is not entirely clear, and so the new s. 106A constitutes a clarification of the breadth of the federal spending power.

Subsection (2) of s. 106A provides that: "Nothing in this section extends the legislative powers of the Parliament of Canada or of the legislatures of the provinces". But subsection (1) makes sense only in the light of the assumptions about the existence of the extensive federal spending power described in the previous paragraph. So subsection (2) must be saying, in effect: The federal power to spend and impose conditions in areas of exclusive provincial jurisdiction has always existed.

National shared-cost program

The constitutional restriction on federal power that is imposed by s. 106A applies only to "a national shared-cost program that is established by the Government of Canada". Any federal policy, including a spending program, that does not take the form of a national shared-cost program is unaffected by s. 106A.

What is a "national" shared-cost program? Clearly, it is one "established by the Government of Canada", as s. 106A explains. As well, a national program would surely have to be one offered to all provinces, not a bilateral program offered to a single province (or several provinces).

The "shared-cost" element of the program would derive from the fact that the program would be funded partly by the federal government and partly by the provincial governments. The national program would take the form of an offer of cash (or "tax points") by the federal government to the provinces for the purpose of partially funding the provision of federally-defined services in each province. The offer would be conditional upon each province (1) applying the federal grant for the stipulated purpose, (2) contributing a share of the cost of the services in that province, and (3) enacting any legislation that was required for the provision of the services and that was within the exclusive competence of the provincial Legislature.

If the federal offer was accepted by a province, and if the province satisfied the conditions, then the national program would operate in that province. If the federal offer was not accepted by the province, or if the province failed to satisfy the conditions, then the national program would not operate in that province and the province would not be entitled to the federal grant. In the latter situation, the effect of s. 106A would be to require the government of Canada to pay "reasonable compensation" to the province, provided that the province establishes a program of its own compatible with the national objectives of the federal program.

Even a national shared-cost program is only caught by s. 106A if two limiting conditions apply. The first condition is that the program must be established "after the coming into force of this section". Thus 106A applies only to new programs, not to existing ones. The second condition is that the program must be established "in an area of exclusive provincial jurisdiction". Thus, 106A would not apply to a shared-cost program in an area of exclusive federal jurisdiction, such as "Indians" (s. 91(24)). Nor would s. 106A apply to a shared-cost program in an area of concurrent federal-provincial jurisdiction, such as "Agriculture" or "Immigration" (s. 95).

National objectives

The obligation to provide reasonable compensation arises only if the non-participating province "carries on a program or initiative that is compatible with the national objectives". It is unfortunate that the phrase "national objectives" was not given clearer definition in the constitutional text. However, in the context of a provision dealing with "a national shared-cost program", it seems plain that the national objectives are the objectives of the national shared-cost program.

How are the objectives of the national shared-cost program to be ascertained? Again, the context suggests an answer. Since the national shared-cost program is "established by the Government of Canada", it seems plain that the objectives established by the government or Parliament of Canada would be accepted by the courts as the objectives of the program. This does not mean that the national objectives would necessarily be set unilaterally by the federal government: from both a legal and a political standpoint it would be desirable to achieve federal-provincial agreement on a statement of national objectives. It seems obvious that a court would defer to a statement of national objectives arrived at by a consensual process. If reasonable national objectives were set unilaterally by the federal government, and articulated in the legislation establishing a program, then I think that a court would accept that articulation as the national objectives. I say "reasonable" national objectives, because the courts will undoubtedly review the Parliament's assertion of the national objectives to be sure that there is an intelligible national rationale for each. The courts will not uncritically accept every picayune point that is asserted in federal legislation as a national objective.

A national objective will always be a rather general proposition, but it may carry detailed specific implications. Take the Canada Health Act as a hypothetical example. (It is hypothetical because s. 106A has no application to shared-cost programs that are already in existence.) If the universal accessiblity of free health care were accepted as a national objective, then the ban on extra-billing would seem to be an essential element of any plan that conformed to the national objectives. In other words, a plan established by a non-participating province that did not include a ban on extra-billing would not be compatible with the national objectives.

Compatibility

Section 106A requires reasonable compensation to be paid to a province that "carries on a program or initiative that is compatible with the national objectives". What does "compatible" mean in this context?

The word "compatible" is defined in the Shorter Oxford English Dictionary as follows:

1. Sympathetic.
2. Mutually tolerant; capable of existing together in the same subject; accordant, consistent, congruous.

It seems to me that the only meaning that makes sense in the context of s. 106A is "sympathetic". The obvious purpose underlying s. 106A is to extend funding to provinces that are pursuing programs with objectives that are sympathetic to, that is, similar to, the objectives of the national program.

If compatible were given a broader meaning, as including anything not directly inconsistent with the national objectives, s. 106A would lack an intelligible purpose. If a national day-care program were established by the federal government, it would make no sense to pay reasonable compensation to a non-participating province that wanted to put the money into public highways (for example). Such a use of the funds would leave day-care unsupported in the non-participating province, and would apply federal funds to an objective which, even if it is "national" in some sense, has never been approved by the federal government, which has the responsibility for disbursing funds raised from all across the country.

I conclude that a provincial program would be "compatible" with the national objectives only if the provincial program pursued essentially the same objectives as those of the national program. What is permitted by s. 106A is some variation in the means by which those objectives are to be achieved. For example, if a national day-care program were established by the federal government, and if it called for assistance to profit-making as well as to not-for-profit day-care centres, a non-participating province might want to limit its program to not-for-profit day-care centres. That is a variation in the means of delivering day-care that might suit the conditions of the province and the ideology of its government better than the national plan. It seems likely to me that the province's plan would be "compatible" with the national objectives of the national plan.

Reasonable compensation

What form must "reasonable compensation" take?

Cash is obviously acceptable. Reasonable compensation could therefore take the form of a cash grant from the federal government to the non-participating provincial government.

What about "tax points"? This is more difficult, because tax points are no more than potential provincial revenue. A grant of tax points to a non-participating province means a lowering of federal tax rates for the residents of the non-participating province so as to make possible an increase in provincial rates. Tax points are now used to adjust revenues between the federal government and the provinces, and are used to compensate Quebec for opting out of existing shared-cost programs. I think "reasonable compensation" will be interpreted against the backdrop of established Canadian federal-provincial fiscal mechanisms, and would be held to include tax points.

Note that s. 106A stipulates that reasonable compensation be provided "to the government of a province". This would preclude the federal government from providing compensation in the form of benefits to individuals. Payments to the residents of the non-participating province, or tax deductions or tax credits for the residents of the province, would not qualify as reasonable compensation.

How much compensation is "reasonable". If the non-participating province is operating a program that is equivalent in cost to the national program, presumably reasonable compensation would consist of whatever the province would have been entitled to had it joined the national program. If the province's program is more costly than the national program, the compensation would still be the same: the discretionary choice to put more provincial resources into a program should not entitle the province to extra federal aid. If the province's program is less costly than the national program, then I think this would react on the amount of compensation that had to be provided. In that case, a lesser sum would be "reasonable". Otherwise, federal funds earmarked for particular national objectives would become available for general provincial purposes.

9

AMENDING FORMULA

Text of ss. 40, 41, 44, 46(1), 47(1)

Clauses 9 to 12 of the schedule to the Meech Lake Constitutional Accord provide as follows:

9. Sections 40 to 42 of the *Constitution Act, 1982* are repealed and the following substituted therefor:

Compensation

40. Where an amendment is made under subsection 38(1) that transfers legislative powers from provincial legislatures to Parliament, Canada shall provide reasonable compensation to any province to which the amendment does not apply.

Amendment by unanimous consent

41. An amendment to the Constitution of Canada in relation to the following matters may be made by proclamation issued by the Governor General under the Great Seal of Canada only where authorized by resolutions of the Senate and House of Commons and of the legislative assembly of each province:

(*a*) the office of the Queen, the Governor General and the Lieutenant Governor of a province;

(*b*) the powers of the Senate and the method of selecting Senators;

(*c*) the number of members by which a province is entitled to be represented in the Senate and the residence qualifications of Senators;

(*d*) The right of a province to a number of members in the House of Commons not less than the number of Senators by which the province was entitled to be represented on April 17, 1982;

(*e*) **The principle of proportionate representation of the provinces in the House of Commons prescribed by the Constitution of Canada;**

(*f*) **subject to section 43, the use of the English or the French language;**

(*g*) **the Supreme Court of Canada;**

(*h*) **the extension of existing provinces into the territories;**

(*i*) **notwithstanding any other law or practice, the establishment of new provinces; and**

(*j*) **an amendment to this Part.**

10. Section 44 of the said Act is repealed and the following substituted therefor:

Amendments by Parliament

44. Subject to section 41, Parliament may exclusively make laws amending the Constitution of Canada in relation to the executive government of Canada or the Senate and House of Commons.

11. Subsection 46(1) of the said Act is repealed and the following substituted therefor:

Initiation of amendment procedures

46. (1) The procedures for amendment under sections 38, 41 and 43 may be initiated either by the Senate or the House of Commons or by the legislative assembly of a province.

12. Subsection 47(1) of the said Act is repealed and the following substituted therefor:

Amendments without Senate resolution

47. (1) An amendment to the Constitution of Canada made by proclamation under section 38, 41 or 43 may be made without a resolution of the Senate authorizing the issue of the proclamation if, within one hundred and eighty days after the adoption by the House of Commons of a resolution authorizing its issue, the Senate has not adopted such a resolution and if, at any time after the expiration of that period, the House of Commons again adopts the resolution.

Summary of changes

The effect of these amendments is to make two changes in the amending procedures.

The first change concerns the right of a province to receive compensation for opting-out of a constitutional amendment. Under the existing version of s. 40 of the Constitution Act, 1982, the right to compensation applies to a transfer from the provincial Legislatures to the federal Parliament of legislative powers relating to education or other cultural matters. The new s. 40 broadens this right to apply to a transfer from the provincial Legislatures to the federal Parliament of any legislative powers, not just those relating to education or other cultural matters.

The second change in the amending procedures concerns the procedure for certain amendments affecting the Senate, the House of Commons, the Supreme Court of Canada, the extension of existing provinces and the establishment of new provinces. At present, s. 42 of the Constitution Act, 1982 enables amendments upon defined aspects of these topics to be made by the seven-province formula of s. 38. The Meech Lake amendments will repeal s. 42. All the matters formerly contained in s. 42 will now be added to a new s. 41, where they will become subject to the unanimity procedure of s. 41.

Quebec veto

The amending procedures that were agreed to by the first ministers, except for Premier Levesque of Quebec, on November 5, 1981, and that became Part V of the Constitution Act, 1982, differed from all previous proposals for amending formulae in one important respect: the Part V procedures did not give a veto to the province of Quebec. That is why one of Quebec's conditions for its willing assent to the Constitution was a veto on constitutional amendments.

Until 1982 it was arguable that Quebec had a "conventional" right to veto significant constitutional amendments. Of course, no province had a "legal" right of veto, because the provinces had no legal role to play in an amending procedure which took the form of a statute of the United Kingdom Parliament enacted at the request of the Canadian (federal) government.

When the constitutional settlement of November 5, 1981 was agreed to by all first ministers, except for Premier Levesque of Quebec, the question of the existence of a conventional veto was put to the test. The federal government on this occasion was not deterred by Quebec's dissent from requesting the agreed-upon amendments from the United Kingdom Parliament, and the United Kingdom Parliament complied with the request by enacting the amendments. Unsuccessful in the political arena, Quebec turned to the courts, directing a reference of the question whether there was a conventional requirement of Quebec's consent to constitutional amendments that affected Quebec's powers. By the time the reference reached the Supreme Court of Canada the question was moot: the enactment by the United Kingdom Parliament had completed the legal formalities, and the Canada Act 1982 and the Constitution Act, 1982 had become law. Nonetheless, the Supreme Court of Canada answered the referred question. The Court held that Quebec did not have a veto on constitutional amendments. The conventional requirements were satisfied if the request by the federal government was supported by a "substantial degree" of provincial consent, and Quebec did not have to be part of a substantial degree of provincial consent: the assent of the nine predominantly English-speaking provinces satisfied the convention. (*Re Objection by Quebec to Resolution to Amend the Constitution* [1982] 2 S.C.R. 793.)

The decision of the Supreme Court of Canada in the *Quebec Veto Reference* did not succeed in erasing a widespread sense of grievance in Quebec. The fact was that a constitutional amendment with profound effects on provincial powers (through the Charter of Rights and amending formula) had been imposed on Quebec against the wishes of its provincial government. It is not surprising, therefore, that when Premier Bourassa opened discussions for a reconciliation of Quebec to the Constitution one of Quebec's conditions was that the new amending procedures be modified to give Quebec a veto.

Opting-out of amendments

Under Part V of the Constitution Act, 1982, the general amending procedure is established by s. 38. Section 38 requires the assent of the federal government (resolutions of the Senate and House of Commons) and of the legislative assemblies of two-thirds of the provinces (seven provinces) representing fifty per cent of the population. This "seven-fifty formula" or "seven-province formula" can be operated without the assent of any one province. Quebec and Ontario together can block an amendment, because their combined populations represent more than fifty per cent of the population of all the provinces. But neither Quebec nor Ontario by itself can block an amendment. In short, s. 38 does not give Quebec (or any other province) a veto.

While s. 38 does not give any one province a veto, it does protect each province from unwanted reductions in its powers by provision for opting-out. Subsection (3) of s. 38 permits a province, by passing a resolution of dissent in its legislative assembly, to opt-out of any amendment "that derogates from the legislative powers, the proprietary rights or any other rights or privileges of the legislature or government of [the] province". If a resolution of dissent is passed by a province, then the amendment will have no effect in that province.

Suppose, for example, that the federal government and seven provinces representing fifty per cent of the population agreed to transfer jurisdiction over prisons (now provincial under s. 92(6)) from the provincial Legislatures to the federal Parliament. Since this amendment would derogate from the legislative powers of the provinces, opting-out would be available under s. 38(3). Any one (or all) of the three non-agreeing provinces could pass the resolution of dissent that would make the amendment ineffective in that province. In an opted-out province, jurisdiction over prisons would continue to be provincial. The new federal legislative power over prisons would not extend throughout the country: it would stop at the borders of the opted-out province.

The power to opt-out is not the same as a veto. A veto blocks an unwanted amendment altogether, that is, for all parts of Canada. Opting-out blocks an unwanted amendment only in the opted-out province: elsewhere in Canada the amendment will take effect. However, opting-out is like a veto in that it operates to shield a province from an unwanted amendment.

Compensation for opting-out

Is opting-out equivalent to a veto as a shield for Quebec against unwanted amendments? The answer is: not quite; and one reason is that opting-out may carry a financial penalty.

The financial penalty may be illustrated by returning to the prisons example.

If Quebec was the only province that opted out of the amendment transferring prisons from provincial to federal jurisdiction, Quebec would continue to operate its prisons, while the federal government would take over the operation of the prisons in the other provinces. This would require Quebec to bear an expense that in the other provinces had been assumed by the federal government. From the point of view of the residents of Quebec, their federal taxes would contribute to the operation of prisons in the rest of the country, and yet they would have to support the Quebec prisons through provincial taxes.

In the negotiations leading up to the 1982 amending formula, it was proposed in the "Vancouver formula" that opting-out should be accompanied by the payment of compensation to the opted-out province. With this addition, the seven-fifty formula was acceptable to Premier Levesque of Quebec, who was one of the eight Premiers supporting the Vancouver formula. (The competing "Victoria formula", propounded by the federal government and two provinces, gave a veto to Quebec.) The final settlement of the amending formula included only a limited right to compensation. Section 40 affords a right to "reasonable compensation" when provincial legislative powers relating to "education or other cultural matters" are transferred from provincial Legislatures to Parliament. If, as in the prisons example, the transferred power does not relate to education or other cultural matters, then the opted-out province has no constitutional right to receive reasonable compensation for its additional expenses.

The Meech Lake Constitutional Accord goes back to the Vancouver formula by removing the limitation on the right to compensation that is now in s. 40. The new s. 40 no longer restricts the right to compensation to transfers of provincial powers over "education or other cultural matters". The new s. 40 applies to any transfer of provincial legislative powers to the federal Parliament: an opting-out province will be entitled to reasonable compensation for the retention of the responsibility that in other provinces has been assumed by the federal government. This extension of the right to compensation removes the financial penalty from opting-out. Opting-out is still not a veto, but opting-out with compensation is regarded by Quebec as a sufficient safeguard against losses of provincial powers.

Where opting-out is unavailable

There are some kinds of amendments which could have an adverse effect on Quebec and from which no opting-out is possible. Changes in central institutions fall into this category. A change in the monarchy, or the Senate, or the House of Commons, or the Supreme Court of Canada would obviously have effect in Quebec. Yet opting-out of a change in central institutions is inherently impossible. One could not have a Senate (for example) composed in one way for nine provinces, and composed differently for Quebec (or any other opted-out province).

The admission of a new province is another example. This would have indirect effects on the other provinces, but opting-out is inherently impossible. A change in the amending procedures themselves is another matter where there cannot be a different rule for an opted-out province. For amendments of these kinds, there is no obvious substitute for a veto for Quebec.

The Constitution Act, 1982, by ss. 41 and 42, dealt with these kinds of inherently national amendments in two ways. Section 41 applied a unanimity formula to five classes of amendments, which were as follows:

    (a) the office of the Queen, the Governor General and the Lieutenant Governor of a province;

    (b) the right of a province to a number of members in the House of Commons not less than the number of Senators by which the province is entitled to be represented at the time this Part comes into force;

    (c) subject to section 43, the use of the English or the French language;

    (d) the composition of the Supreme Court of Canada; and

    (e) an amendment to this Part.

Section 42 applied the general seven-fifty formula to six classes of amendments, which were as follows:

    (a) the principle of proportionate representation of the provinces in the House of Commons prescribed by the Constitution of Canada;

    (b) the powers of the Senate and the method of selecting Senators;

    (c) the number of members by which a province is entitled to be represented in the Senate and the residence qualifications of Senators;

    (d) subject to paragraph 41(d), the Supreme Court of Canada;

    (e) the extension of existing provinces into the territories; and

    (f) notwithstanding any other law or practice, the establishment of new provinces.

The unanimity formula of s. 41 requires the assent of the federal government and all provinces. For those amendments, each province has a veto, since any province's failure to give assent would block the amendment. Therefore, with respect to the five s. 41 categories, Quebec has a veto. However, with respect to the six s. 42 categories, the seven-fifty formula does not require the assent of Quebec, and opting-out is specifically forbidden by s. 42(2). With respect to those categories, therefore, Quebec is unprotected either by a veto or by the power to opt-out.

Expansion of unanimity formula

The Meech Lake Constitutional Accord introduces a new s. 41 to the Constitution Act, 1982. The new s. 41 is enlarged to include all the categories that were formerly in s. 42. The enlarged new s. 41 thus applies the unanimity formula to the old-s. 42 categories as well as the old-s. 41 categories. Old s. 42, having been robbed of all content by new s. 41, is to be repealed. In this way, the Accord shifts the s. 42 categories out of the seven-fifty column and into the unanimity column. The requirement of unanimity gives Quebec a veto.

The extension of the unanimity formula by the expansion of s. 41 was no doubt the only practicable way to give a veto to Quebec without abandoning the principle of the equality of the provinces. It has the unfortunate effect of making the amending procedures even more rigid and difficult to operate than they were before Meech Lake. On the other hand, the Meech Lake Accord itself demonstrates that unanimity is not unattainable, where meetings of first ministers are preceded by thorough preparation and where there is a general desire to achieve a settlement. It is also worth noting that the matters listed in the new s. 41 encompass for the most part matters with sufficiently profound potential effects on the nation as a whole that there is a plausible argument in favour of the unanimity requirement.

The most controversial of the items that are moved into the unanimity column by the new s. 41 is "the establishment of new provinces" (new s. 41(i)). It has been pointed out that this change will make it more difficult for the two northern territories to achieve provincial status. Obviously, this is true. It is also true that before the Constitution Act, 1982 a new province could be carved out of a federal territory by the unilateral action of the federal Parliament: Constitution Act, 1871, ss. 2, 5; and this is how Manitoba, Alberta and Saskatchewan were created. It is also arguable that the existing provinces have no legitimate concern with the devolution to the territories of province-like powers of internal self-government. Nevertheless, when devolution reaches the stage of full provincial status, the other provinces are profoundly, albeit indirectly, affected. The establishment of new provinces would increase the total number of provinces and thus indirectly affect the operation of the amending formula. Since any direct amendment of the amending formula now requires unanimity (old s. 41(e)), it is arguable that other amendments having the same effect ought to be subject to the same requirement. Another point is that the establishment of new provinces, especially provinces with sparse populations, large territories and harsh climates, would entail a substantial revision of the federal-provincial financial arrangements. This is another topic upon which unanimity is at least desirable. It follows that a case can be made for the proposition that all existing provinces should agree to the introduction of new provinces.

Consequential amendments

The new ss. 44, 46 and 47(1) that are substituted by clauses 10, 11 and 12 of the schedule to the Meech Lake Constitutional Accord are not changed in any substantive way from their predecessors. They are simply redrafted to recognize the disappearance of s. 42, which, it will be recalled, was repealed by clause 9 of the Accord.

10

FIRST MINISTERS' CONFERENCES

Text of ss. 148, 50

Clause 8 of the schedule to the Meech Lake Constitutional Accord adds a new s. 148 at the end of the Constitution Act, 1867. The new s. 148 provides as follows:

Conferences on the economy and other matters

148. A conference composed of the Prime Minister of Canada and the first ministers of the provinces shall be convened by the Prime Minister of Canada at least once each year to discuss the state of the Canadian economy and such other matters as may be appropriate.

Clause 13 of the schedule to the Meech Lake Constitutional Accord repeals Part VI of the Constitution Act, 1982 (which contained ss. 50 and 51), and introduces a new s. 50, which provides as follows:

Constitutional conference

50. (1) A constitutional conference composed of the Prime Minister of Canada and the first ministers of the provinces shall be convened by the Prime Minister of Canada at least once each year, commencing in 1988.

Agenda

(2) The conferences convened under subsection (1) shall have included on their agenda the following matters:

(a) Senate reform, including the role and functions of the Senate, its powers, the method of selecting Senators and representation in the Senate;

(b) roles and responsibilities in relation to fisheries; and

(c) such other matters as are agreed upon.

Summary of changes

The new s. 148 of the Constitution Act, 1867 requires that a conference of first ministers be held "at least once a year" in order "to discuss the state of the Canadian economy and such other matters as may be appropriate".

The new s. 50 of the Constitution Act, 1982 requires that a "constitutional conference" of first ministers be convened by the Prime Minister "at least once each year, commencing in 1988". The agenda for these conferences has to include Senate reform and fisheries. There is no time limit on the operation of s. 50. It requires that constitutional conferences be held every year without any limit of time, and that the same two items be included on the agenda of every meeting.

Constitutional reform

It seems odd to include in the Constitution a requirement that a form of constitutional convention meet each year without any limit of time, and that the same two items be included on the agenda of every meeting. Changing the Constitution is a stressful and time-consuming exercise which should be attempted only occasionally, and only when there is reason to believe in the likelihood of success. I speculate that new s. 50, although couched in permanent form, is really intended to be temporary. It is designed to guarantee that the process of constitutional discussion will move on to topics that were set aside at Meech Lake so as not to complicate unduly the paramount goal of securing Quebec's assent to the Constitution Act, 1982. Now that the "Quebec round" has been successfully completed, the proponents of Senate reform and fisheries reform have an assurance that their concerns will also be addressed. Presumably, if agreements can be reached on those topics, new s. 50 would be amended, at least to take the topics off the permanent agenda, and, perhaps, to eliminate the requirement of annual meetings. Indeed, if agreement cannot be reached, consideration should be given to modifying or repealing s. 50 so that it does not continue to mandate a futile enterprise.

The technique of requiring future constitutional conferences to carry on with unfinished business was also used in the Constitution Act, 1982. Section 37 required that a constitutional conference of the first ministers be held within one year of April 17, 1982 (the coming into force of the Constitution Act, 1982), and s. 37 required that the agenda include aboriginal rights. That meeting was held in 1983, with the participation of aboriginal representatives, and it agreed upon some changes to s. 35 (aboriginal rights) which have since been formally implemented: Constitution Amendment Proclamation, 1983. At the same time the now spent s. 37 was repealed and a new s. 37.1 was introduced into the Act calling for "at least two" more constitutional conferences on the topic of aboriginal rights. Since that stipulation was agreed to, there have been three such conferences, but no agreement has been reached on any amendment to the Constitution. The primary objective of the aboriginal peoples at these conferences was to obtain a constitutional guarantee of self-government. That objective has not been realized. It seems likely, however, that, along with the Senate and the fishery, aboriginal self-government will be one of the matters considered at future constitutional conferences. (See *Report* of the Special Joint Committee on the 1987 Constitutional Accord (1987), ch. XI.)

First ministers' conferences

The Meech Lake Constitutional Accord is not the first time that first ministers' conferences have been entrenched in the Constitution. As explained in the previous section, s. 37 of the Constitution Act, 1982 made provision for a first ministers' conference, and s. 37.1 (added in 1983) made substituted provision for such conferences. As well, s. 49 of the Constitution Act, 1982 requires a constitutional conference of first ministers to meet within fifteen years of April 17, 1982 to review the amending formula. These provisions, now supplemented by the new ss. 148 and 50 to be added by Meech Lake, give constitutional recognition to first ministers' conferences.

A conference of first ministers is composed of only eleven people: the Prime Minister of Canada and the ten Premiers of the provinces. All eleven people are of course elected officials, who are accountable to their legislative bodies and, ultimately, to their electorates. Even so, at first blush, the group seems to be too small and too narrowly composed to serve as a constitutional convention. But the reality is that the evolution of responsible government in Canada has concentrated extraordinary power in the hands of these eleven first ministers. The Prime Minister owes his position to his leadership of the party that commands a majority of seats in the House of Commons. That majority, which accepts a rigid regime of party discipline, normally enables the Prime Minister to control the legislative process in the Parliament. Each provincial Premier is in the same position in his province: the Premier is normally able to control the legislative process of his province.

The first ministers, when they meet, bring together the totality of executive power and (in effect) legislative power. They are able to make commitments to each other of executive or legislative action which they are in a position to carry out. (No American president or state governor possesses comparable powers.) It is not surprising, therefore, that the first ministers' conferences have developed into a regular forum in which federal-provincial arrangements of various kinds, including financial arrangements, are settled. First ministers' conferences have been important institutions in Canada for many years, although until 1982 they were not mentioned in the Constitution.

The amending procedures of Part V of the Constitution Act, 1982 are operated by resolutions of the Senate and House of Commons at the federal level, and by resolutions of the legislative assemblies at the provincial level. Since these bodies are normally effectively controlled by the eleven first ministers, the obvious way of making them act in concert is by agreement of the first ministers. It is therefore only a slight exaggeration to say that in Canada constituent power resides with the eleven first ministers. This is the reality that the Constitution now implicitly acknowledges. The Special Joint Committee, seeking to broaden participation in the constituent process, proposed the establishment of a federal-provincial constitutional committee composed of representatives of the federal, provincial and territorial governments. The function of this committee would be to prepare the ground for each constitutional conference of first ministers by holding public hearings, receiving submissions and making recommendations on constitutional proposals before final decisions were made by the first ministers (*Report* of the Special Joint Committee on the 1987 Constitutional Accord (1987), 134).

APPENDICES

Appendix I

MEECH LAKE COMMUNIQUE
OF APRIL 30, 1987

At their meeting today at Meech Lake, the Prime Minister and the ten Premiers agreed to ask officials to transform into a constitutional text the agreement in principle found in the attached document.

First Ministers also agreed to hold a constitutional conference within weeks to approve a formal text intended to allow Quebec to resume its place as a full participant in Canada's constitutional development.

QUEBEC'S DISTINCT SOCIETY

(1) The Constitution of Canada shall be interpreted in a manner consistent with

   a) the recognition that the existence of French-speaking Canada, centred in but not limited to Quebec, and English-speaking Canada, concentrated outside Quebec but also present in Quebec, constitutes a fundamental characteristic of Canada; and

   b) the recognition that Quebec constitutes within Canada a distinct society.

(2) Parliament and the provincial legislatures, in the exercise of their respective powers, are committed to preserving the fundamental characteristic of Canada referred to in paragraph (1)(a).

(3) The role of the legislature and Government of Quebec to preserve and promote the distinct identity of Quebec referred to in paragraph (1)(b) is affirmed.

Appendice I

COMMUNIQUÉ DU LAC MEECH
LE 30 AVRIL 1987

Réunis aujourd'hui en conférence au Lac Meech, le Premier ministre du Canada et les premiers ministres des dix provinces canadiennes sont convenus de donner instruction à des légistes de traduire en un texte constitutionnel l'entente de principe qui se trouve dans le document ci-joint.

Ils sont également convenus de tenir d'ici quelques semaines une conférence constitutionnelle pour sanctionner un texte formel visant à permettre au Québec de reprendre sa place, à part entière, dans l'évolution constitutionnelle canadienne.

CARACTÈRE DISTINCT DU QUÉBEC

(1) L'interprétation de la Constitution du Canada doit concorder avec

   a) la reconnaissance que l'existence d'un Canada francophone, concentré mais non limité au Québec, et celle d'un Canada anglophone, concentré dans le reste du pays mais présent au Québec, constituent une caractéristique fondamentale de la fédération canadienne;

   b) la reconnaissance que le Québec forme au sein du Canada une société distincte.

(2) Le Parlement et les législatures des provinces, dans l'exercice de leurs compétences respectives, prennent l'engagement de protéger la caractéristique fondamentale du Canada mentionnée au paragraphe (1)a).

(3) L'Assemblée nationale et le gouvernement du Québec ont le rôle de protéger et de promouvoir le caractère distinct de la société québécoise mentionné au paragraphe (1)b).

IMMIGRATION

— Provide under the Constitution that the Government of Canada shall negotiate an immigration agreement appropriate to the needs and circumstances of a province that so requests and that, once concluded, the agreement may be entrenched at the request of the province;

— such agreements must recognize the federal government's power to set national standards and objectives relating to immigration, such as the ability to determine general categories of immigrants, to establish overall levels of immigration and prescribe categories of inadmissible persons;

— under the foregoing provisions, conclude in the first instance an agreement with Quebec that would:

  • incorporate the principles of the Cullen-Couture agreement on the selection abroad and in Canada of independent immigrants, visitors for medical treatment, students and temporary workers, and on the selection of refugees abroad and economic criteria for family reunification and assisted relatives;

  • guarantee that Quebec will receive a number of immigrants, including refugees, within the annual total established by the federal government for all of Canada proportionate to its share of the population of Canada, with the right to exceed that figure by 5% for demographic reasons; and

  • provide an undertaking by Canada to withdraw services (except citizenship services) for the reception and integration (including linguistic and cultural) of all foreign nationals wishing to settle in Quebec where services are to be provided by Quebec, with such withdrawal to be accompanied by reasonable compensation;

— nothing in the foregoing should be construed as preventing the negotiation of similar agreements with other provinces.

SUPREME COURT OF CANADA

— Entrench the Supreme Court and the requirement that at least three of the nine justices appointed be from the civil bar;

— provide that, where there is a vacancy on the Supreme Court, the federal government shall appoint a person from a list of candidates proposed by the provinces and who is acceptable to the federal government.

SPENDING POWER

— Stipulate that Canada must provide reasonable compensation to any province that does not participate in a future national shared-cost program in an area of exclusive provincial jurisdiction if that province undertakes its own initiative

IMMIGRATION

— Prévoir dans la Constitution qu'à la requête d'une province, le gouvernement du Canada négociera, en matière d'immigration, une entente qui réponde aux besoins et aux circonstances particulières de cette province et pourra, sur demande, la constitutionnaliser une fois conclue;

— établir l'obligation de reconnaître dans ces ententes le pouvoir du gouvernement fédéral de fixer des normes et des objectifs nationaux en matière d'immigration, en particulier son droit de définir les catégories générales d'immigrants, d'établir les niveaux globaux d'immigration et de désigner comme inadmissibles certaines catégories de personnes;

— préciser qu'en vertu des dispositions qui précèdent, le gouvernement fédéral conclura en premier lieu avec le Québec une entente qui:

• incorporera les principes de l'entente Cullen-Couture en ce qui concerne la sélection à l'étranger et au pays des immigrants indépendants, des visiteurs admis pour soins médicaux, des étudiants et des travailleurs temporaires, et la sélection des réfugiés à l'étranger ainsi que les critères économiques régissant la réunification des familles et les parents aidés;

• garantira au Québec, à l'intérieur du total annuel établi par le gouvernement fédéral pour l'ensemble du Canada, un nombre d'immigrants, incluant les réfugiés, proportionnel à sa part de la population canadienne, avec droit de dépasser ce chiffre de 5 pour cent pour des raisons démographiques; et

• engagera le Canada à se retirer de tout service (à l'exception des services relatifs à la citoyenneté) en matière de réception et d'intégration (y compris l'intégration linguistique et culturelle) des ressortissants étrangers, lorsque des services sont fournis par le Québec, pareil retrait devant s'accompagner d'une juste compensation;

— rien dans la présente ne saurait empêcher la négociation d'ententes semblables avec d'autres provinces.

COUR SUPRÊME DU CANADA

— Constitutionnaliser la Cour suprême ainsi que l'obligation de nommer au moins trois de ses neuf juges à même le Barreau civil;

— stipuler qu'advenant une vacance à la Cour suprême, le gouvernement fédéral nommera, à même une liste de noms proposés par les provinces, une personne dont la candidature lui agrée.

POUVOIR DE DÉPENSER

— Stipuler que le Canada doit accorder une juste compensation à toute province qui ne participe pas à un nouveau programme national à frais partagés dans un domaine de compétence provinciale exclusive si cette province met en oeuvre

on programs compatible with national objectives.

AMENDING FORMULA

— Maintain the current general amending formula set out in section 38, which requires the consent of Parliament and at least two-thirds of the provinces representing at least fifty percent of the population;

— guarantee reasonable compensation in all cases where a province opts out of an amendment transferring provincial jurisdiction to Parliament;

— because opting out of constitutional amendments to matters set out in section 42 of the *Constitution Act, 1982* is not possible, require the consent of Parliament and all the provinces for such amendments.

SECOND ROUND

— Require that a First Ministers' Conference on the Constitution be held not less than once per year and that the first be held within twelve months of proclamation of this amendment but not later than the end of 1988;

— entrench in the Constitution the following items on the agenda:

1) Senate reform including:

— the functions and role of the Senate;

— the powers of the Senate;

— the method of selection of Senators;

— the distribution of Senate seats;

2) fisheries roles and responsibilities; and

3) other agreed upon matters;

— entrench in the Constitution the annual First Ministers' Conference on the Economy now held under the terms of the February 1985 Memorandum of Agreement;

— until constitutional amendments regarding the Senate are accomplished the federal government shall appoint persons from lists of candidates provided by provinces where vacancies occur and who are acceptable to the federal government.

de son propre chef une initiative ou un programme compatible avec les objectifs nationaux.

FORMULE DE MODIFICATION

— Maintenir la formule générale de modification constitutionnelle prévue actuellement à l'article 38, qui exige le consentement du Parlement et celui des assemblées législatives d'au moins deux tiers des provinces représentant au moins cinquante pour cent de la population;

— accorder une compensation raisonnable dans tous les cas où une province se dissocie d'une modification portant transfert d'une compétence provinciale au Parlement;

— étant donné l'impossibilité de se dissocier d'une modification touchant les questions énumérées à l'article 42 de la *Loi constitutionnelle de 1982*, exiger à cet égard le consentement du Parlement et de toutes les provinces.

DEUXIÈME RONDE

— Rendre obligatoire la tenue au moins chaque année d'une Conférence des premiers ministres sur la Constitution, la première devant avoir lieu dans les 12 mois suivant la proclamation de la présente modification constitutionnelle, au plus tard d'ici la fin de 1988;

— inscrire dans la Constitution les points suivants à l'ordre du jour:

1) la réforme du Sénat, notamment:

— les fonctions et le rôle du Sénat;

— les pouvoirs du Sénat;

— le mode de sélection des sénateurs;

— la répartition des sièges au Sénat;

2) les rôles et les responsabilités en matière de pêche; et

3) toute autre question dont on aura convenu;

— consacrer dans la Constitution la Conférence annuelle des premiers ministres sur l'économie prévue actuellement par le Protocole d'entente de février 1985;

— tant que la Constitution n'aura pas été modifiée en ce qui concerne le Sénat, le gouvernement fédéral nommera, à même une liste de noms proposés par la province où une vacance se produit, une personne dont la candidature lui agrée.

Appendix II

1987 CONSTITUTIONAL ACCORD

WHEREAS first ministers, assembled in Ottawa, have arrived at a unanimous accord on constitutional amendments that would bring about the full and active participation of Quebec in Canada's constitutional evolution, would recognize the principle of equality of all the provinces, would provide new arrangements to foster greater harmony and cooperation between the Government of Canada and the governments of the provinces and would require that annual first ministers' conferences on the state of the Canadian economy and such other matters as may be appropriate be convened and that annual constitutional conferences composed of first ministers be convened commencing not later than December 31, 1988;

AND WHEREAS first ministers have also reached unanimous agreement on certain additional commitments in relation to some of those amendments;

NOW THEREFORE the Prime Minister of Canada and the first ministers of the provinces commit themselves and the governments they represent to the following:

1. The Prime Minister of Canada will lay or cause to be laid before the Senate and House of Commons, and the first ministers of the provinces will lay or cause to be laid before their legislative assemblies, as soon as possible, a resolution, in the form appended hereto, to authorize a proclamation to be issued by the Governor General under the Great Seal of Canada to amend the Constitution of Canada.

2. The Government of Canada will, as soon as possible, conclude an agreement with the Government of Quebec that would

(*a*) incorporate the principles of the Cullen-Couture agreement on the selection abroad and in Canada of independent immigrants, visitors for medical treatment, students, and temporary workers, and on the selection of refugees abroad and economic criteria for family reunification and assisted relatives.

Appendice II

ACCORD CONSTITUTIONNEL DE 1987

Les premiers ministres du Canada et des provinces, considérant :

qu'à leur réunion d'Ottawa, ils ont conclu à l'unanimité un accord sur des modifications constitutionnelles propres à assurer la participation peine et entière du Québec à l'évolution constitutionnelle du Canada dans le respect du principe de l'égalité de toutes les provinces et, par de nouveaux arrangements, à renforcer l'harmonie et la coopération entre le gouvernement du Canada et ceux des provinces, ainsi que sur la tenue de conférences annuelles des premiers ministres sur l'économie canadienne et sur toute autre question appropriée et de conférences constitutionnelles annuelles des premiers ministres, la première devant avoir lieu le 31 décembre 1988 au plus tard;

qu'ils ont pris, à l'unanimité également, des engagements complémentaires à propos de certaines de ces modifications,

prennent, en leur propre nom et en celui des gouvernements qu'ils représentent, les engagements suivants :

1. Les premiers ministres du Canada et des provinces déposeront ou feront déposer respectivement devant le Sénat et la Chambre des communes et devant les assemblées législatives, dans les meilleurs délais, la résolution dont le texte figure en annexe et autorisant la modification de la Constitution du Canada par proclamation du gouverneur général sous le grand sceau du Canada.

2. Dans les meilleurs délais, le gouvernement du Canada conclura avec celui du Québec une entente qui :

(*a*) incorporera les principes de l'entente Cullen-Couture en ce qui concerne la sélection à l'étranger et au Canada des immigrants indépendants, des visiteurs admis pour soins médicaux, des étudiants et des travailleurs temporaires, et la sélection des réfugiés à l'étranger ainsi que les critères économiques régissant la réunification des familles et les parents aidés;

(*b*) guarantee that Quebec will receive a number of immigrants, including refugees, within the annual total established by the federal government for all of Canada proportionate to its share of the population of Canada, with the right to exceed that figure by five per cent for demographic reasons, and

(*c*) provide an undertaking by Canada to withdraw services (except citizenship services) for the reception and integration (including linguistic and cultural) of all foreign nationals wishing to settle in Quebec where services are to be provided by Quebec, with such withdrawal to be accompanied by reasonable compensation,

and the Government of Canada and the Government of Quebec will take the necessary steps to give the agreement the force of law under the proposed amendment relating to such agreements.

3.   Nothing in this Accord should be construed as preventing the negotiation of similar agreements with other provinces relating to immigration and the temporary admission of aliens.

4. Until the proposed amendment relating to appointments to the Senate comes into force, any person summoned to fill a vacancy in the Senate shall be chosen from among persons whose names have been submitted by the government of the province to which the vacancy relates and must be acceptable to the Queen's Privy Council for Canada.

(*b*) garantira au Québec, sur le total annuel établi par le gouvernement fédéral pour l'ensemble du Canada, un nombre d'immigrants, y compris les réfugiés, proportionnel à sa part de la population canadienne, avec droit de dépasser ce chiffre de cinq pour cent pour des raisons démographiques;

(*c*) engagera le Canada à retirer les services — à l'exception de ceux qui sont relatifs à la citoyenneté — de réception et d'intégration, y compris l'intégration linguistique et culturelle, des ressortissants étrangers désireux de s'établir au Québec lorsque des services sont fournis par le Québec, pareil retrait devant s'accompagner d'une juste compensation.

Le gouvernement du Canada et celui du Québec prendront ensuite les mesures nécessaires pour donner, conformément au projet de modification, force de loi à l'entente.

3. Le présent accord ne saurait empêcher la négociation d'ententes semblables avec d'autres provinces en matière d'immigration et d'admission temporaire des ressortissants étrangers.

4. Jusqu'à l'entrée en vigueur de la modification relative aux nominations au Sénat, les personnes nommées aux sièges vacants au Sénat seront choisies parmi celles qui auront été proposées par le gouvernement de la province à représenter et agréées par le Conseil privé de la Reine pour le Canada.

Appendix III

MOTION FOR A RESOLUTION TO AUTHORIZE AN AMENDMENT TO THE CONSTITUTION OF CANADA

WHEREAS the *Constitution Act, 1982* came into force on April 17, 1982, following an agreement between Canada and all the provinces except Quebec;

AND WHEREAS the Government of Quebec has established a set of five proposals for constitutional change and has stated that amendments to give effect to those proposals would enable Quebec to resume a full role in the constitutional councils of Canada;

AND WHEREAS the amendment proposed in the schedule hereto sets out the basis on which Quebec's five constitutional proposals may be met;

AND WHEREAS the amendment proposed in the schedule hereto also recognizes the principle of the equality of all the provinces, provides new arrangements to foster greater harmony and cooperation between the Government of Canada and the governments of the provinces and requires that conferences be convened to consider important constitutional, economic and other issues;

AND WHEREAS certain portions of the amendment proposed in the schedule hereto relate to matters referred to in section 41 of the *Constitution Act, 1982*;

AND WHEREAS section 41 of the *Constitution Act, 1982* provides that an amendment to the Constitution of Canada may be made by proclamation issued by the Governor General under the Great Seal of Canada where so authorized by resolutions of the Senate and the House of Commons and of the legislative assembly of each province;

NOW THEREFORE the (Senate) (House of Commons) (legislative assembly) resolves that an amendment to the Constitution of Canada be authorized to be made by proclamation issued by Her Excellency the Governor General under the Great Seal of Canada in accordance with the schedule hereto.

Appendice III

MOTION DE RÉSOLUTION AUTORISANT LA MODIFICATION DE LA CONSTITUTION DU CANADA

Attendu :

que la *Loi constitutionnelle de 1982* est entrée en vigueur le 17 avril 1982, à la suite d'un accord conclu entre le Canada et toutes les provinces, sauf le Québec;

que, selon le gouvernement du Québec, l'adoption de modifications visant à donner effet à ses cinq propositions de révision constitutionnelle permettrait au Québec de jouer pleinement de nouveau son rôle dans les instances constitutionnelles canadiennes;

que le projet de modification figurant en annexe présente les modalités d'un règlement relatif aux cinq propositions du Québec;

que le projet reconnaît le principe de l'égalité de toutes les provinces et prévoit, d'une part, de nouveaux arrangements propres à renforcer l'harmonie et la coopération entre le gouvernement du Canada et ceux des provinces, d'autre part la tenue de conférences consacrées à l'étude d'importantes questions constitutionnelles, économiques et autres;

que le projet porte en partie sur des questions visées à l'article 41 de la *Loi constitutionnelle de 1982*;

que cet article prévoit que la Constitution du Canada peut être modifiée par proclamation du gouverneur général sous le grand sceau du Canada, autorisée par des résolutions du Sénat, de la Chambre des communes et de l'assemblée législative de chaque province,

(le Sénat) (la Chambre des communes) (l'assemblée législative) a résolu d'autoriser la modification de la Constitution du Canada par proclamation de Son Excellence le gouverneur général sous le grand sceau du Canada, en conformité avec l'annexe ci-jointe.

Appendix IV

SCHEDULE

CONSTITUTION AMENDMENT, 1987

Constitution Act, 1867

1. The *Constitution Act, 1867* is amended by adding thereto, immediately after section 1 thereof, the following section:

Interpretation

2. (1) The Constitution of Canada shall be interpreted in a manner consistent with

(*a*) the recognition that the existence of French-speaking Canadians, centred in Quebec but also present elsewhere in Canada, and English-speaking Canadians, concentrated outside Quebec but also present in Quebec, constitutes a fundamental characteristic of Canada; and

(*b*) the recognition that Quebec constitutes within Canada a distinct society.

Role of Parliament and legislatures

(2) The role of the Parliament of Canada and the provincial legislatures to preserve the fundamental characteristics of Canada referred to in paragraph (1)(*a*) is affirmed.

Role of legislature and Government of Quebec

(3) The role of the legislature and Government of Quebec to preserve and promote the distinct identity of Quebec referred to in paragraph (1)(*b*) is affirmed.

Rights of legislatures and governments preserved

(4) Nothing in this section derogates from the powers, rights or privileges of Parliament or the Government of Canada, or of the legislatures or governments of the prov-

Appendice IV

ANNEXE

MODIFICATION CONSTITUTIONNELLE DE 1987

Loi constitutionnelle de 1867

1. La *Loi constitutionnelle de 1867* est modifiée par insertion, après l'article 1, de ce qui suit :

Règle interprétative   **2.** (1) Toute interprétation de la Constitution du Canada doit concorder avec :

a) la reconnaissance de ce que l'existence de Canadiens d'expression française, concentrés au Québec mais présents aussi dans le reste du pays, et de Canadiens d'expression anglaise, concentrés dans le reste du pays mais aussi présents au Québec, constitue une caractéristique fondamentale du Canada;

b) la reconnaissance de ce que le Québec forme au sein du Canada une société distincte.

Rôle du Parlement et des législatures   (2) Le Parlement du Canada et les législatures des provinces ont le rôle de protéger la caractéristique fondamentale du Canada visée à l'alinéa (1)*a*).

Rôle de la législature et du gouvernement du Québec   (3) La législature et le gouvernement du Québec ont le rôle de protéger et de promouvoir le caractère distinct du Québec visé à l'alinéa (1)*b*).

Maintien des droits des législatures et gouvernements   (4) Le présent article n'a pas pour effet de déroger aux pouvoirs, droits ou privilèges du Parlement ou du gouvernement du Canada, ou des législatures ou des gouvernements

inces, including any powers, rights or privileges relating to language.

2. The said Act is further amended by adding thereto, immediately after section 24 thereof, the following section:

Names to be submitted

25. (1) Where a vacancy occurs in the Senate, the government of the province to which the vacancy relates may, in relation to that vacancy, submit to the Queen's Privy Council for Canada the names of persons who may be summoned to the Senate.

Choice of Senators from names submitted

(2) Until an amendment to the Constitution of Canada is made in relation to the Senate pursuant to section 41 of the *Constitution Act, 1982*, the person summoned to fill a vacancy in the Senate shall be chosen from among persons whose names have been submitted under subsection (1) by the government of the province to which the vacancy relates and must be acceptable to the Queen's Privy Council for Canada.

3. The said Act is further amended by adding thereto, immediately after section 95 thereof, the following heading and sections:

Agreements on Immigration and Aliens

Commitment to negotiate

95A. The Government of Canada shall, at the request of the government of any province, negotiate with the government of that province for the purpose of concluding an agreement relating to immigration or the temporary admission of aliens into that province that is appropriate to the needs and circumstances of that province.

Agreements

95B. (1) Any agreement concluded between Canada and a province in relation to immigration or the temporary admission of aliens into that province has the force of law from the time it is declared to do so in accordance with subsection 95C(1) and shall from that time have effect notwithstanding class 25 of section 91 or section 95.

Limitation

(2) An agreement that has the force of law under subsection (1) shall have effect only so long and so far as it is not repugnant to any provision of an Act of the Parliament of Canada that sets national standards and objectives relating to immigration or aliens, including any provision that establishes general classes of immigrants or relates to levels of immigration for Canada or that prescribes classes of individuals who are inadmissible into Canada.

des provinces, y compris à leurs pouvoirs, droits ou privilèges en matière de langue.

2. La même loi est modifiée par insertion, après l'article 24, de ce qui suit :

Propositions

25. (1) En cas de vacance au Sénat, le gouvernement de la province à représenter peut proposer au Conseil privé de la Reine pour le Canada des personnes susceptibles d'être nommées au siège vacant.

Choix des sénateurs

(2) Jusqu'à la modification, faite conformément à l'article 41 de la *Loi constitutionnelle de 1982*, de toute disposition de la Constitution du Canada relative au Sénat, les personnes nommées aux sièges vacants au Sénat sont choisies parmi celles qui ont été proposées par le gouvernement de la province à représenter et agréées par le Conseil privé de la Reine pour le Canada.

3. La même loi est modifiée par insertion, après l'article 95, de ce qui suit :

Accords relatifs à l'immigration et aux aubains

Engagement

95A. Sur demande du gouvernement d'une province, le gouvernement du Canada négocie avec lui en vue de conclure, en matière d'immigration ou d'admission temporaire des aubains dans la province, un accord adapté aux besoins et à la situation particulière de celle-ci.

Accords

95B. (1) Tout accord conclu entre le Canada et une province en matière d'immigration ou d'admission temporaire des aubains dans la province a, une fois faite la déclaration visée au paragraphe 95C(1), force de loi et a dès lors effet indépendamment tant du point 25 de l'article 91 que de l'article 95.

Restriction

(2) L'accord ayant ainsi force de loi n'a d'effet que dans la mesure de sa compatibilité avec les dispositions des lois du Parlement du Canada qui fixent des normes et objectifs nationaux relatifs à l'immigration et aux aubains, notamment en ce qui concerne l'établissement des catégories générales d'immigrants, les niveaux d'immigration du Canada et la détermination des catégories de personnes inadmissibles au Canada.

Application of Charter

(3) The *Canadian Charter of Rights and Freedoms* applies in respect of any agreement that has the force of law under subsection (1) and in respect of anything done by the Parliament or Government of Canada, or the legislature or government of a province, pursuant to any such agreement.

Proclamation relating to agreements

95C. (1) A declaration that an agreement referred to in subsection 95B(1) has the force of law may be made by proclamation issued by the Governor General under the Great Seal of Canada only where so authorized by resolutions of the Senate and House of Commons and of the legislative assembly of the province that is a party to the agreement.

Amendment of agreements

(2) An amendment to an agreement referred to in subsection 95B(1) may be made by proclamation issued by the Governor General under the Great Seal of Canada only where so authorized

(*a*) by resolutions of the Senate and House of Commons and of the legislative assembly of the province that is a party to the agreement; or

(*b*) in such other manner as is set out in the agreement.

Application of sections 46 to 48 of Constitution Act, 1982

95D. Sections 46 to 48 of the *Constitution Act, 1982* apply, with such modifications as the circumstances require, in respect of any declaration made pursuant to subsection 95C(1), any amendment to an agreement made pursuant to subsection 95C(2) or any amendment made pursuant to section 95E.

Amendments to sections 95A to 95D or this section

95E. An amendment to sections 95A to 95D or this section may be made in accordance with the procedure set out in subsection 38(1) of the *Constitution Act, 1982*, but only if the amendment is authorized by resolutions of the legislative assemblies of all the provinces that are, at the time of the amendment, parties to an agreement that has the force of law under subsection 95B(1).

4. The said Act is further amended by adding thereto, immediately preceding section 96 thereof, the following heading:

General

5. The said Act is further amended by adding thereto, immediately preceding section 101 thereof, the following heading:

Application de la Charte

(3) La *Charte canadienne des droits et libertés* s'applique aux accords ayant ainsi force de loi et à toute mesure prise sous leur régime par le Parlement ou le gouvernement du Canada ou par la législature ou le gouvernement d'une province.

Proclamation relative aux accords

95C. (1) La déclaration portant qu'un accord visé au paragraphe 95B(1) a force de loi se fait par proclamation du gouverneur général sous le grand sceau du Canada, autorisée par des résolutions du Sénat, de la Chambre des communes et de l'assemblée législative de la province qui est partie à l'accord.

Modification des accords

(2) La modification d'un accord visé au paragraphe 95B(1) se fait par proclamation du gouverneur général sous le grand sceau du Canada, autorisée :

a) soit par des résolutions du Sénat, de la Chambre des communes et de l'assemblée législative de la province qui est partie à l'accord;

b) soit selon les modalités prévues dans l'accord même.

Application des articles 46 à 48 de la *Loi constitutionnelle de 1982*

95D. Les articles 46 à 48 de la *Loi constitutionnelle de 1982* s'appliquent, avec les adaptations nécessaires, à toute déclaration faite aux termes du paragraphe 95C(1), à toute modification d'un accord faite aux termes du paragraphe 95C(2) ou à toute modification faite aux termes de l'article 95E.

Modification des articles 95A à 95D ou du présent article

95E. Les articles 95A à 95D ou le présent article peuvent être modifiés conformément au paragraphe 38(1) de la *Loi constitutionnelle de 1982*, à condition que la modification soit autorisée par des résolutions des assemblées législatives de toutes les provinces qui sont, à l'époque de celle-ci, parties à un accord ayant force de loi aux termes du paragraphe 95B(1).

4. La même loi est modifiée par insertion, avant l'article 95, de ce qui suit :

Dispositions générales

5. La même loi est modifiée par insertion, avant l'article 101, de ce qui suit :

Courts Established by the Parliament of Canada

6. The said Act is further amended by adding thereto, immediately after section 101 thereof, the following heading and sections:

Supreme Court of Canada

Supreme Court continued

101A. (1) The court existing under the name of the Supreme Court of Canada is hereby continued as the general court of appeal for Canada, and as an additional court for the better administration of the laws of Canada, and shall continue to be a superior court of record.

Constitution of court

(2) The Supreme Court of Canada shall consist of a chief justice to be called the Chief Justice of Canada and eight other judges, who shall be appointed by the Governor General in Council by letters patent under the Great Seal.

Who may be appointed judges

101B. (1) Any person may be appointed a judge of the Supreme Court of Canada who, after having been admitted to the bar of any province or territory, has, for a total of at least ten years, been a judge of any court in Canada or a member of the bar of any province or territory.

Three judges from Quebec

(2) At least three judges of the Supreme Court of Canada shall be appointed from among persons who, after having been admitted to the bar of Quebec, have, for a total of at least ten years, been judges of any court of Quebec or of any court established by the Parliament of Canada, or members of the bar of Quebec.

Names may be submitted

101C. (1) Where a vacancy occurs in the Supreme Court of Canada, the government of each province may, in relation to that vacancy, submit to the Minister of Justice of Canada the names of any of the persons who have been admitted to the bar of that province and are qualified under section 101B for appointment to that court.

Appointment from names submitted

(2) Where an appointment is made to the Supreme Court of Canada, the Governor General in Council shall, except where the Chief Justice is appointed from among members of the Court, appoint a person whose name has been submitted under subsection (1) and who is acceptable to the Queen's Privy Council for Canada.

Appointment from Quebec

(3) Where an appointment is made in accordance with subsection (2) of any of the three judges necessary to meet the requirement set out in subsection 101B(2), the Governor General in Council shall appoint a person whose name has been submitted by the Government of Quebec.

Tribunaux créés par le Parlement du Canada

6. La même loi est modifiée par insertion, après l'article 101, de ce qui suit :

Cour suprême du Canada

Maintien de la Cour suprême du Canada

101A. (1) La cour qui existe sous le nom de Cour suprême du Canada est maintenue à titre de cour générale d'appel pour le Canada et de cour additionnelle propre à améliorer l'application des lois du Canada. Elle conserve ses attributions de cour supérieure d'archives.

Composition

(2) La Cour suprême du Canada se compose du juge en chef, appelé juge en chef du Canada, et de huit autres judges, que nomme le gouverneur général en conseil par lettres patentes sous le grand sceau.

Conditions de nomination

101B. (1) Les juges sont choisis parmi les personnes qui, après avoir été admises au barreau d'une province ou d'un territoire, ont, pendant au moins dix ans au total, été juges de n'importe quel tribunal du pays ou inscrites au barreau de n'importe quelle province ou de n'importe quel territoire.

Québec : trois juges

(2) Au moins trois des juges sont choisis parmi les personnes qui, après avoir été admises au barreau du Québec, ont, pendant au moins dix ans au total, été inscrites à ce barreau ou juges d'un tribunal du Québec ou d'un tribunal créé par le Parlement du Canada.

Propositions de nomination

101C. (1) En cas de vacance à la Cour suprême du Canada, le gouvernement de chaque province peut proposer au ministre fédéral de la Justice, pour la charge devenue vacante, des personnes admises au barreau de cette province et remplissant les conditions visées à l'article 101B.

Nomination parmi les personnes proposées

(2) Le gouverneur général en conseil procède aux nominations parmi les personnes proposées et qui agréént au Conseil privée de la Reine pour le Canada; le présent paragraphe ne s'applique pas à la nomination du juge en chef dans le cas où il est choisi parmi les juges de la Cour suprême du Canada.

Nomination parmi les personnes proposées par le Québec

(3) Dans le cas de chacune des trois nominations à faire conformément au paragraphe 101B(2), le gouverneur général en conseil nomme une personne proposée par le gouvernement du Québec.

Appointment from other provinces

(4) Where an appointment is made in accordance with subsection (2) otherwise than as required under subsection (3), the Governor General in Council shall appoint a person whose name has been submitted by the government of a province other than Quebec.

Tenure, salaries, etc., of judges

101D. Sections 99 and 100 apply in respect of the judges of the Supreme Court of Canada.

Relationship to section 101

101E. (1) Sections 101A to 101D shall not be construed as abrogating or derogating from the powers of the Parliament of Canada to make laws under section 101 except to the extent that such laws are inconsistent with those sections.

References to the Supreme Court of Canada

(2) For greater certainty, section 101A shall not be construed as abrogating or derogating from the powers of the Parliament of Canada to make laws relating to the reference of questions of law or fact, or any other matters, to the Supreme Court of Canada.

7. The said Act is further amended by adding thereto, immediately after section 106 thereof, the following section:

Shared-cost program

106A. (1) The Government of Canada shall provide reasonable compensation to the government of a province that chooses not to participate in a national shared-cost program that is established by the Government of Canada after the coming into force of this section in an area of exclusive provincial jurisdiction, if the province carries on a program or initiative that is compatible with the national objectives.

Legislative power not extended

(2) Nothing in this section extends the legislative powers of the Parliament of Canada or of the legislatures of the provinces.

8. The said Act is further amended by adding thereto the following heading and sections:

XII—CONFERENCES ON THE ECONOMY AND OTHER MATTERS

Conferences on the economy and other matters

148. A conference composed of the Prime Minister of Canada and the first ministers of the provinces shall be convened by the Prime Minister of Canada at least once each year to discuss the state of the Canadian economy and such other matters as may be appropriate.

Nominations parmi les personnes proposées par les autres provinces

(4) Dans le cas de toute autre nomination, le gouverneur général en conseil nomme une personne proposée par le gouvernement d'une autre province que le Québec.

Inamovibilité, traitement, etc.

101D. Les articles 99 et 100 s'appliquent aux juges de la Cour suprême du Canada.

Rapport avec l'article 101

101E. (1) Sous réserve que ne soient pas adoptées, dans le matières visées à l'article 101, de dispositions incompatibles avec les articles 101A à 101D, ceux-ci n'ont pas pour effet de porter atteinte à la compétence législative conférée au Parlement du Canada en ces matières.

Renvois à la Cour suprême du Canada

(2) Il est entendu que l'article 101A n'a pas pour effet de porter atteinte à la compétence législative du Parlement du Canada en ce qui concerne le renvoi à la Cour suprême du Canada des questions de droit ou de fait, ou de toute autre question.

7. La même loi est modifiée par insertion, après l'article 106, de ce qui suit :

Programmes cofinancés

106A. (1) Le gouvernement du Canada fournit une juste compensation au gouvernement d'une province qui choisit de ne pas participer à un programme national cofinancé qu'il établit après l'entrée en vigueur du présent article dans un secteur de compétence exclusive provinciale, si la province applique un programme ou une mesure compatible avec les objectifs nationaux.

Non-élargissement des compétences législatives

(2) Le présent article n'élargit pas les compétences législatives du Parlement du Canada ou des législatures des provinces.

8. La même loi est modifiée par insertion, après l'article 147, de ce qui suit :

XII.—Conférences sur l'économie et sur d'autres questions

Convocation

148. Le premier ministre du Canada convoque au moins une fois par an une conférence réunissant les premiers ministres provinciaux et lui-même et portant sur l'économie canadienne ainsi que sur toute autre question appropriée.

XIII—REFERENCES

Reference includes
amendments

149. A reference to this Act shall be deemed to include a reference to any amendments thereto.

Constitution Act, 1982

9. Sections 40 to 42 of the *Constitution Act, 1982* are repealed and the following substituted therefor:

Compensation

40. Where an amendment is made under subsection 38(1) that transfers legislative powers from provincial legislatures to Parliament, Canada shall provide reasonable compensation to any province to which the amendment does not apply.

Amendment by
unanimous consent

41. An amendment to the Constitution of Canada in relation to the following matters may be made by proclamation issued by the Governor General under the Great Seal of Canada only where authorized by resolutions of the Senate and House of Commons and of the legislative assembly of each province:

(*a*) the office of the Queen, the Governor General and the Lieutenant Governor of a province;

(*b*) the powers of the Senate and the method of selecting Senators;

(*c*) the number of members by which a province is entitled to be represented in the Senate and the residence qualifications of Senators;

(*d*) the right of a province to a number of members in the House of Commons not less than the number of Senators by which the province was entitled to be represented on April 17, 1982;

(*e*) the principle of proportionate representation of the provinces in the House of Commons prescribed by the Constitution of Canada;

(*f*) subject to section 43, the use of the English or the French language;

(*g*) the Supreme Court of Canada;

(*h*) the extension of existing provinces into the territories;

(*i*) notwithstanding any other law or practice, the establishment of new provinces; and

(*j*) an amendment to this Part.

XIII.—MENTIONS

Présomption

149. Toute mention de la présente loi est réputée constituer également une mention de ses modifications.

Loi constitutionnelle de 1982

9. Les articles 40 à 42 de la *Loi constitutionnelle de 1982* sont abrogés et remplacés par ce qui suit :

Compensation

40. Le Canada fournit une juste compensation aux provinces auxquelles ne s'applique pas une modification faite conformément au paragraphe 38(1) et relative à un transfert de compétences législatives provinciales au Parlement.

Consentement unanime

41. Toute modification de la Constitution du Canada portant sur les questions suivantes se fait par proclamation du gouverneur général sous le grand sceau du Canada, autorisée par des résolutions du Sénat, de la Chambre des communes et de l'assemblée législative de chaque province :

a) la charge de Reine, celle de gouverneur général et celle de lieutenant-gouverneur;

b) les pouvoirs du Sénat et le mode de sélection des sénateurs;

c) le nombre des sénateurs par lesquels une province est habilitée à être représentée et les conditions de résidence qu'ils doivent remplir;

d) le droit d'une province d'avoir à la Chambre des communes un nombre de députés au moins égal à celui des sénateurs par lesquels elle était habilitée à être représentée le 17 avril 1982;

e) le principe de la représentation proportionnelle des provinces à la Chambre des communes prévu par la Constitution du Canada;

f) sous réserve de l'article 43, l'usage du français ou de l'anglais;

g) la Cour suprême du Canada;

h) le rattachement aux provinces existantes de tout ou partie des territoires;

i) par dérogation à toute autre loi ou usage, la création de provinces;

j) la modification de la présente partie.

10. Section 44 of the said Act is repealed and the following substituted therefor:

Amendments by
Parliament

44. Subject to section 41, Parliament may exclusively make laws amending the Constitution of Canada in relation to the executive government of Canada or the Senate and House of Commons.

11. Subsection 46(1) of the said Act is repealed and the following substituted therefor:

Initiation of amend-
ment procedures

46. (1) The procedures for amendment under sections 38, 41 and 43 may be initiated either by the Senate or the House of Commons or by the legislative assembly of a province.

12. Subsection 47(1) of the said Act is repealed and the following substituted therefor:

Amendments with-
out Senate resolution

47. (1) An amendment to the Constitution of Canada made by proclamation under section 38, 41 or 43 may be made without a resolution of the Senate authorizing the issue of the proclamation if, within one hundred and eighty days after the adoption by the House of Commons of a resolution authorizing its issue, the Senate has not adopted such a resolution and if, at any time after the expiration of that period, the House of Commons again adopts the resolution.

13. Part VI of the said Act is repealed and the following substituted therefor:

PART VI

CONSTITUTIONAL CONFERENCES

Constitutional con-
ference

50. (1) A constitutional conference composed of the Prime Minister of Canada and the first ministers of the provinces shall be convened by the Prime Minister of Canada at least once each year, commencing in 1988.

Agenda

(2) The conferences convened under subsection (1) shall have included on their agenda the following matters:

(*a*) Senate reform, including the role and functions of the Senate, its powers, the method of selecting Senators and representation in the Senate;

(*b*) roles and responsibilities in relation to fisheries; and

(*c*) such other matters as are agreed upon.

14. Subsection 52(2) of the said Act is amended by striking out the word "and" at the end of paragraph (*b*) thereof, by adding the word "and" at the end of paragraph (*c*) thereof and by adding thereto the following paragraph:

10. L'article 44 de la même loi est abrogé et remplacé par ce qui suit :

Modification par le Parlement

44. Sous réserve de l'article 41, le Parlement a compétence exclusive pour modifier les dispositions de la Constitution du Canada relatives au pouvoir exécutif fédéral, au Sénat ou à la Chambre des communes.

11. Le paragraphe 46(1) de la même loi est abrogé et remplacé par ce qui suit :

Initiative des procédures

46. (1) L'initiative des procédures de modification visées aux articles 38, 41 et 43 appartient au Sénat, à la Chambre des communes ou à une assemblée législative.

12. Le paragraphe 47(1) de la même loi est abrogé et remplacé par ce qui suit :

Modification sans résolution du Sénat

47. (1) Dans les cas visés à l'article 38, 41 ou 43, il peut être passé outre au défaut d'autorisation du Sénat si celui-ci n'a pas adopté de résolution dans un délai de cent quatre-vingts jours suivant l'adoption de celle de la Chambre des communes et si cette dernière, après l'expiration du délai, adopte une nouvelle résolution dans le même sens.

13. La partie VI de la même loi est abrogée et remplacée par ce qui suit :

PARTIE VI

CONFÉRENCES CONSTITUTIONNELLES

Convocation

50. (1) Le premier ministre du Canada convoque au moins une fois par an une conférence constitutionnelle réunissant les premiers ministres provinciaux et lui-même, la première devant avoir lieu en 1988.

Ordre du jour

(2) Sont placées à l'ordre du jour de ces conférences les questions suivantes :

a) la réforme du Sénat, y compris son rôle et ses fonctions, ses pouvoirs, le mode de sélection des sénateurs et la représentation au Sénat;

b) les rôles et les responsabilités en matière de pêches;

c) toutes autres questions dont il est convenu.

14. Le paragraphe 52(2) de la même loi est modifié par adjonction de ce qui suit :

(*d*) any other amendment to the Constitution of Canada.

15. Section 61 of the said Act is repealed and the following substituted therefor:

References

61. A reference to the *Constitution Act, 1982*, or a reference to the *Constitution Acts 1867 to 1982*, shall be deemed to include a reference to any amendments thereto.

General

Multicultural heritage and aboriginal peoples

16. Nothing in section 2 of the *Constitution Act, 1867* affects section 25 or 27 of the *Canadian Charter of Rights and Freedoms*, section 35 of the *Constitution Act, 1982* or class 24 of section 91 of the *Constitution Act, 1867*.

CITATION

Citation

17. This amendment may be cited as the *Constitution Amendment, 1987*.

d) les autres modifications qui lui sont apportées.

15. L'article 61 de la même loi est abrogé et remplacé par ce qui suit :

Mentions

61. Toute mention de la *Loi constitutionnelle de 1982* ou des *Lois constitutionnelles de 1867 à 1982* est réputée constituer également une mention de leurs modifications.

Dispositions générales

Patrimoine multiculturel et peuples autochtones

16. L'article 2 de la *Loi constitutionnelle de 1867* n'a pas pour effet de porter atteinte aux articles 25 ou 27 de la *Charte canadienne des droits et libertés*, à l'article 35 de la *Loi constitutionnelle de 1982* ou au point 24 de l'article 91 de la *Loi constitutionnelle de 1867*.

TITRE

Titre

17. Titre de la présente modification : *Modification constitutionnelle de 1987.*

Signed at Ottawa,
June 3, 1987

Fait à Ottawa
le 3 juin 1987

Canada

Ontario

Québec

Nova Scotia
Nouvelle-Écosse

New Brunswick
Nouveau-Brunswick

Manitoba

British Columbia
Colombie-Britannique

Prince Edward Island
Île-du-Prince-Édouard

Saskatchewan

Alberta

Newfoundland
Terre-Neuve

Signed at Ottawa,
June 3, 1987

Fait à Ottawa
le 3 juin 1987

Canada

Ontario

Québec

Nova Scotia
Nouvelle-Écosse

New Brunswick
Nouveau-Brunswick

Manitoba

British Columbia
Colombie-Britannique

Prince Edward Island
Île-du-Prince-Édouard

Saskatchewan

Alberta

Newfoundland
Terre-Neuve